TAYLOR SWIFT
reputation

EASY GUITAR
WITH NOTES & TAB

ISBN 978-1-5400-1342-2

Hal • Leonard®
7777 W. BLUEMOUND RD. P.O. BOX 13819 MILWAUKEE, WI 53213

In Australia Contact:
Hal Leonard Australia Pty. Ltd.
4 Lentara Court
Cheltenham, Victoria, 3192 Australia
Email: ausadmin@halleonard.com.au

Visit Hal Leonard Online at
www.halleonard.com

STRUM AND PICK PATTERNS

This chart contains the suggested strum and pick patterns that are referred to by number at the beginning of each song in this book. The symbols ⊓ and ∨ in the strum patterns refer to down and up strokes, respectively. The letters in the pick patterns indicate which right-hand fingers play which strings.

p = thumb
i = index finger
m = middle finger
a = ring finger

For example; Pick Pattern 2
is played: thumb - index - middle - ring

Strum Patterns   ## Pick Patterns

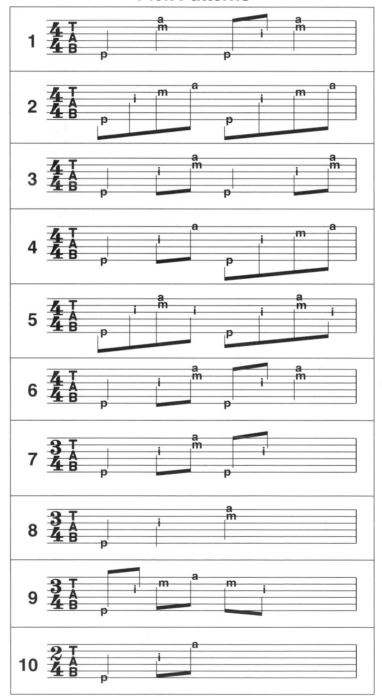

You can use the 3/4 Strum and Pick Patterns in songs written in compound meter (6/8, 9/8, 12/8, etc.).
For example, you can accompany a song in 6/8 by playing the 3/4 pattern twice in each measure.
The 4/4 Strum and Pick Patterns can be used for songs written in cut time (¢) by doubling the note time values in the patterns. Each pattern would therefore last two measures in cut time.

...Ready for It?

Words and Music by Taylor Swift, Max Martin, Shellback and Ali Payami

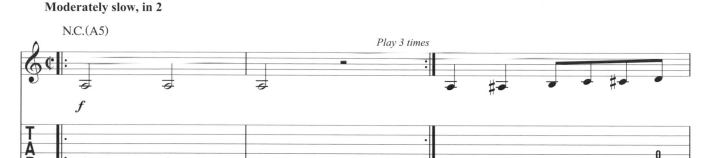

*Capo VII

Strum Pattern: 3
Pick Pattern: 3

Intro
    Moderately slow, in 2

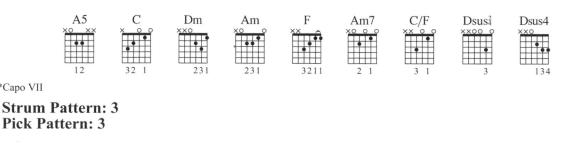

*Optional: To match recording, place capo at 7th fret.

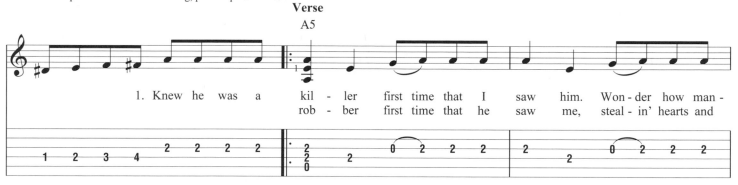

1. Knew he was a kil-ler first time that I saw him. Won-der how man-
rob-ber first time that he saw me, steal-in' hearts and

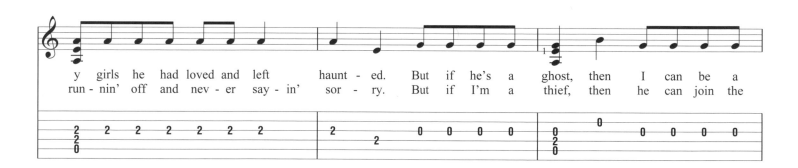

y girls he had loved and left haunt-ed. But if he's a ghost, then I can be a
run-nin' off and nev-er say-in' sor-ry. But if I'm a thief, then he can join the

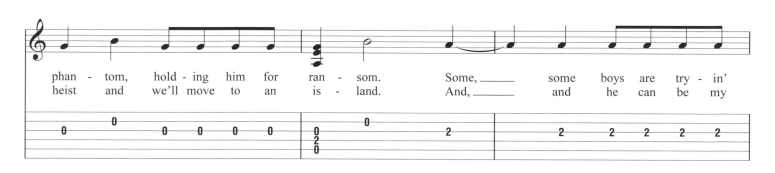

phan-tom, hold-ing him for ran-som. Some, _____ some boys are try-in'
heist and we'll move to an is-land. And, _____ and he can be my

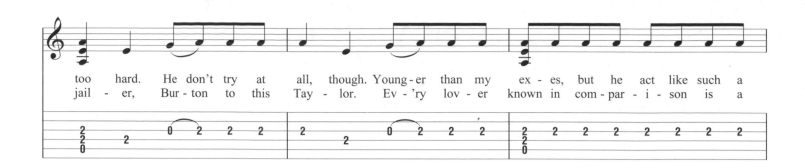

too hard. He don't try at all, though. Young-er than my ex-es, but he act like such a
jail - er, Bur-ton to this Tay - lor. Ev -'ry lov - er known in com - par - i - son is a

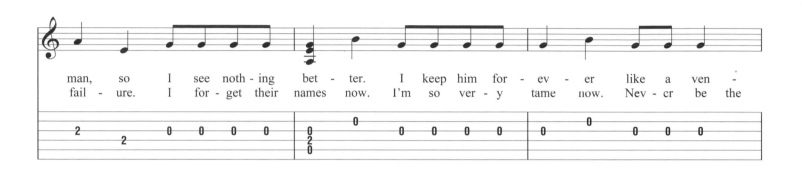

man, so I see noth-ing bet - ter. I keep him for - ev - er like a ven -
fail - ure. I for-get their names now. I'm so ver - y tame now. Nev - er be the

Pre-Chorus

A5

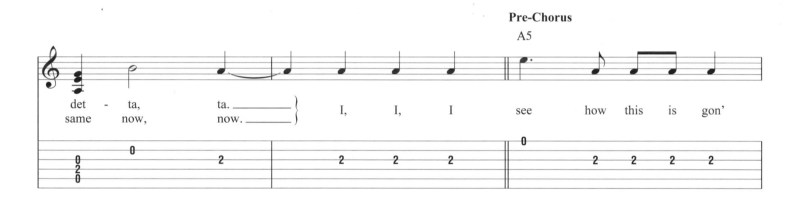

det - ta, ta. _____ I, I, I see how this is gon'
same now, now. _____

go. Touch me and you'll nev - er be a - lone. I, is - land

breeze and lights down low. No one has to know. _____

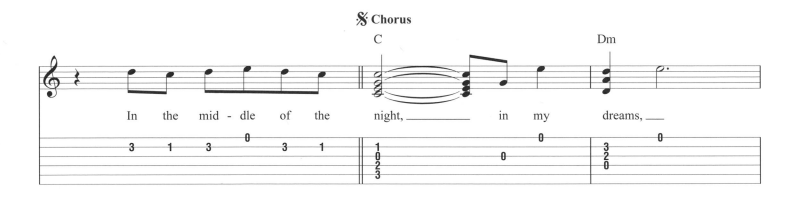

In the mid-dle of the night, _____ in my dreams, ___

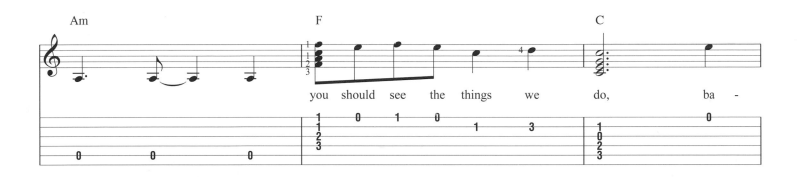

you should see the things we do, ba -

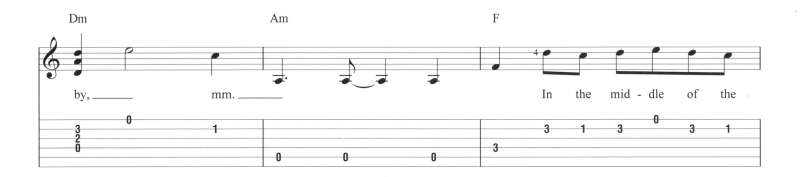

by, _____ mm. _____ In the mid-dle of the

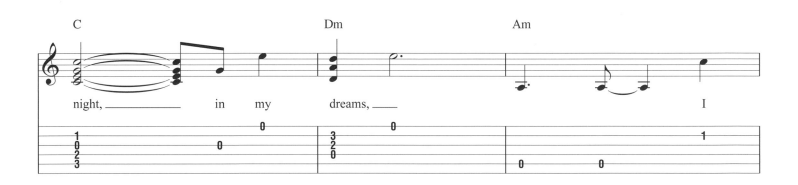

night, _____ in my dreams, ___ I

3rd time, To Coda ⊕

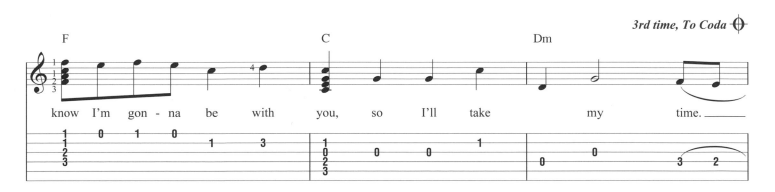

know I'm gon-na be with you, so I'll take my time. ___

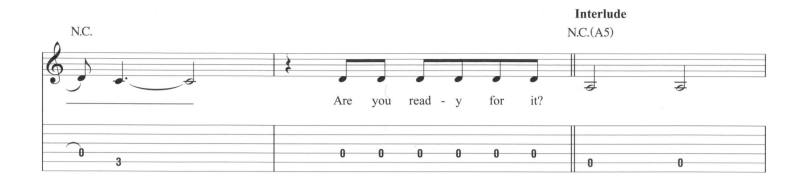

N.C.

Interlude

N.C.(A5)

Are you read - y for it?

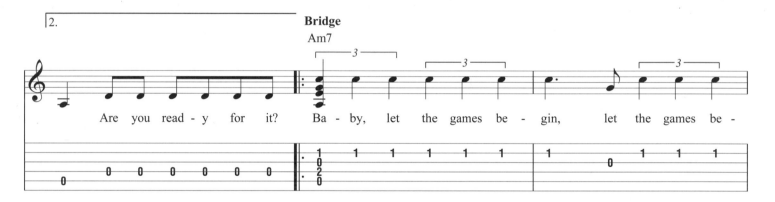

1.

2. Knew I was a

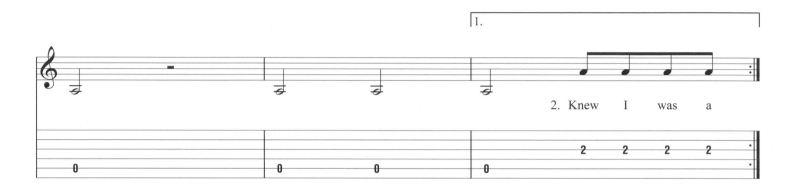

2.

Bridge

Am7

Are you read - y for it? Ba - by, let the games be - gin, let the games be -

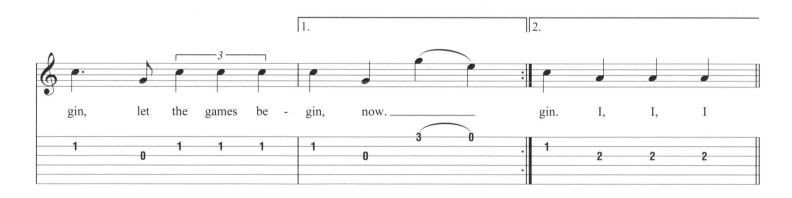

1.   2.

gin, let the games be - gin, now. _____ gin. I, I, I

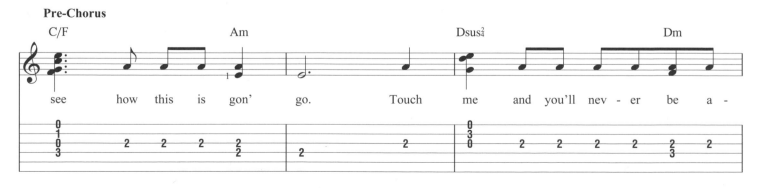

Pre-Chorus

C/F   Am   Dsus²₄   Dm

see how this is gon' go. Touch me and you'll nev - er be a -

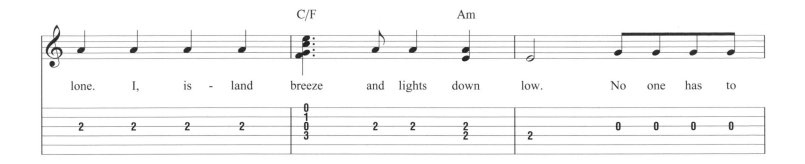

lone. I, is - land breeze and lights down low. No one has to

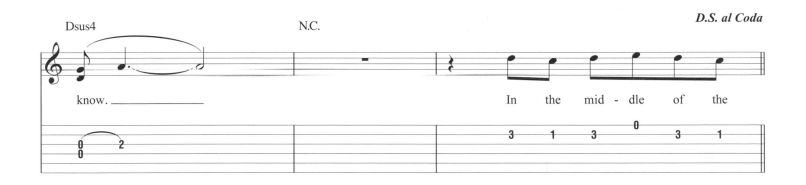

D.S. al Coda

know. _____ In the mid - dle of the

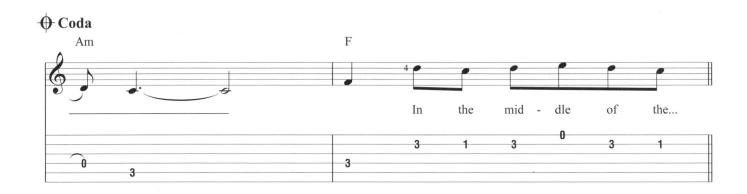

Coda

In the mid - dle of the...

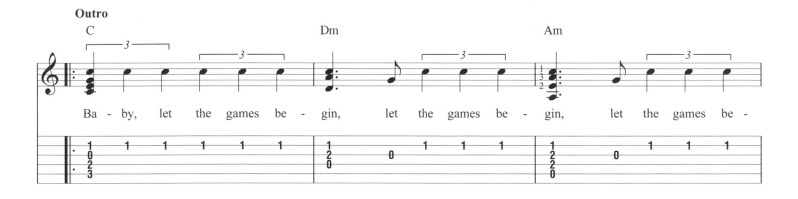

Outro

Ba - by, let the games be - gin, let the games be - gin, let the games be -

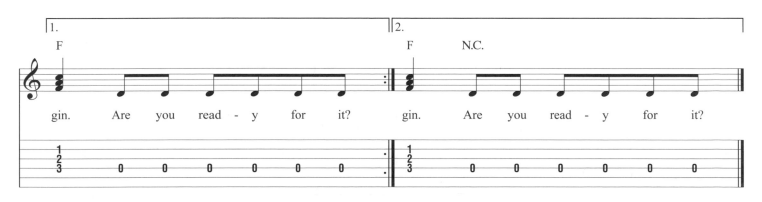

gin. Are you read - y for it? gin. Are you read - y for it?

End Game

Words and Music by Taylor Swift, Ed Sheeran, Max Martin, Shellback and Nayvadius Wilburn

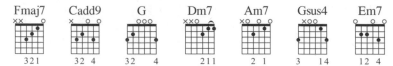

Strum Pattern: 3
Pick Pattern: 3

Chorus
Moderately slow, in 2

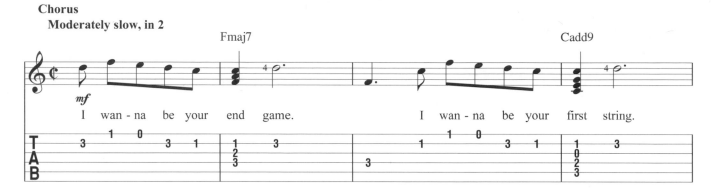

I wan-na be your end game. I wan-na be your first string.

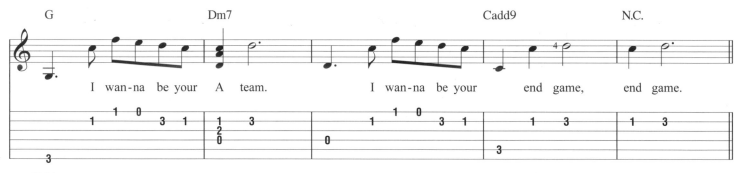

I wan-na be your A team. I wan-na be your end game, end game.

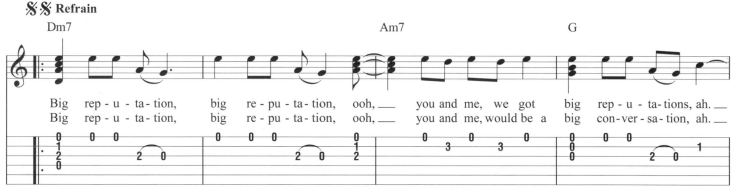

Big rep-u-ta-tion, big re-pu-ta-tion, ooh, ___ you and me, we got big rep-u-ta-tions, ah. ___
Big rep-u-ta-tion, big re-pu-ta-tion, ooh, ___ you and me, would be a big con-ver-sa-tion, ah. ___

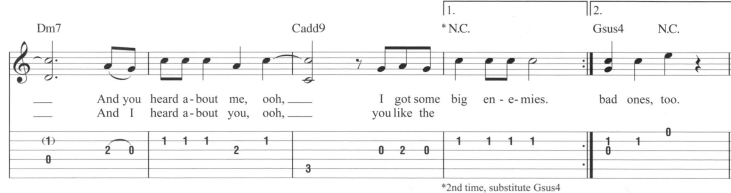

___ And you heard a-bout me, ooh, ___ I got some big en-e-mies. bad ones, too.
___ And I heard a-bout you, ooh, ___ you like the

*2nd time, substitute Gsus4

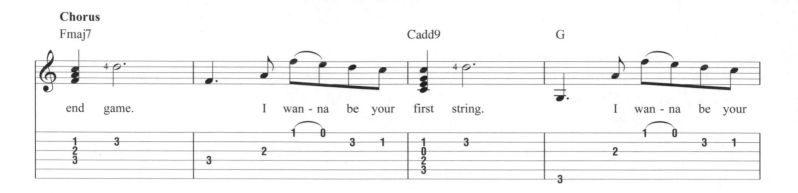

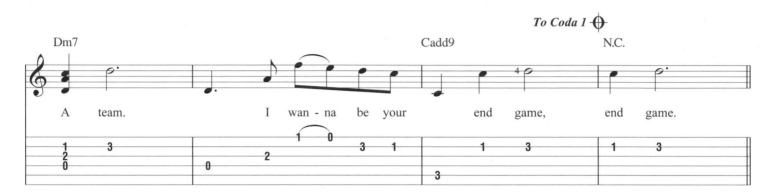

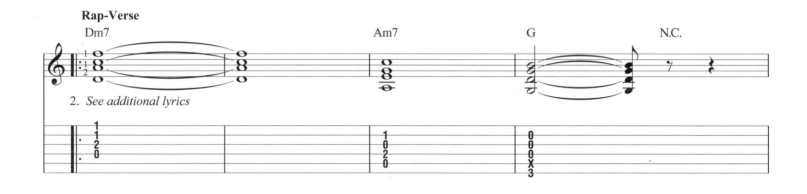

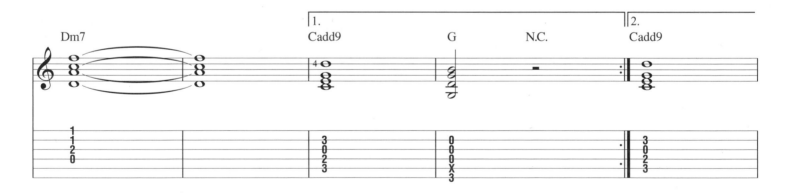

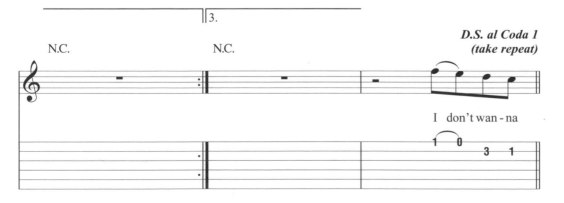

⊕ **Coda 2**

Outro-Chorus

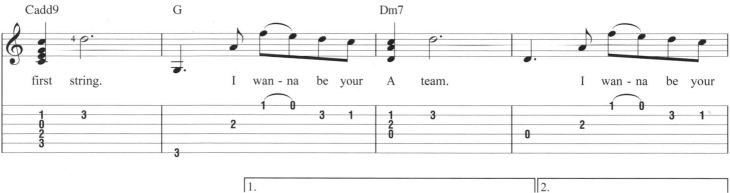

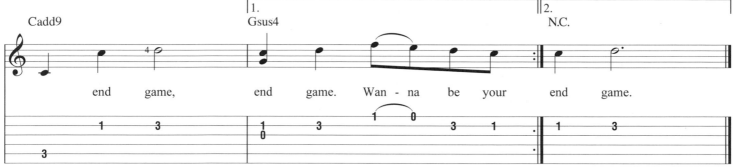

Additional Lyrics

1. *You so dope; don't overdose. I'm so stoked; I need a toast.*
   We do the most, I'm in the ghost like I'm whippin' a boat.
   I got a reputation, girl, that don't precede me.
   I'm a call away whenever you need me.
   I'm in a G5 'cause of the A side.
   I got a bad boy persona; that's what they like.
   You love it.
   I love it, too, 'cause you my type.
   You hold me down and I'll protect you with my life.

2. *Now, well, when I was young, we connected.*
   When we were little bit older, both sprung.
   I got issues and chips on both of my shoulders.
   Reputation precedes me, and rumors are knee-deep.
   The truth is, it's easier to ignore it, believe me.
   Even when we'd argue, we'd not do it for long.
   And you understand the good and bad end up in this song.
   For all your beautiful traits and the way you do it with ease,
   For all my flaws, paranoia and insecurities.
   I've made mistakes and made some choices; that's hard to deny.
   After the storm, something was born on the Fourth of July.
   I've passed days without fun; this end game is the one,
   With four words on the tip of my tongue I'll never say.

3. *I hit you like bang. We tried to forget it, but we just couldn't.*
   And I bury hatchets, but I keep maps of where I put 'em.
   Reputation precedes me; they told you I'm crazy.
   I swear I don't love the drama; it loves me.
   And I can't let you go; your hand-print's on my soul.
   It's like your eyes are liquor, it's like your body is gold.
   You've been calling my bluff on all my usual tricks,
   So here's the truth from my red lips:

I Did Something Bad

Words and Music by Taylor Swift, Max Martin and Shellback

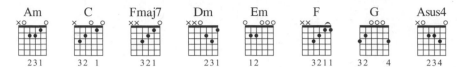

*Tune down 1 step:
(low to high) D-G-C-F-A-D

Strum Pattern: 5
Pick Pattern: 5

Intro
Moderately slow, in 2

*Optional: To match recording, tune down 1 step.

Verse

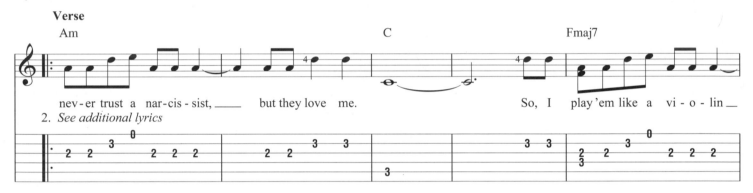

nev-er trust a nar-cis-sist, ___ but they love me. So, I play 'em like a vi-o-lin ___
2. *See additional lyrics*

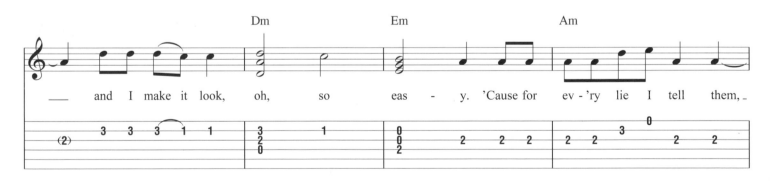

___ and I make it look, oh, so eas-y. 'Cause for ev-'ry lie I tell them, they tell me three.

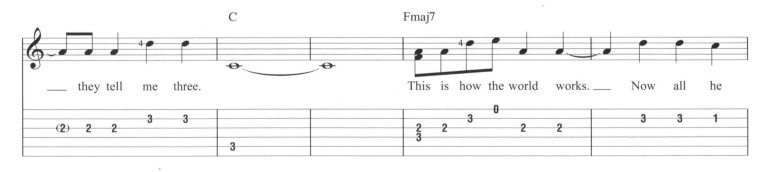

___ they tell me three. This is how the world works. ___ Now all he

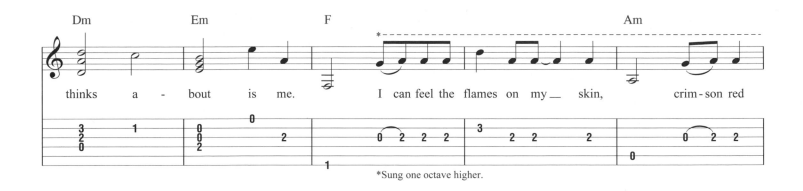

*Sung one octave higher.

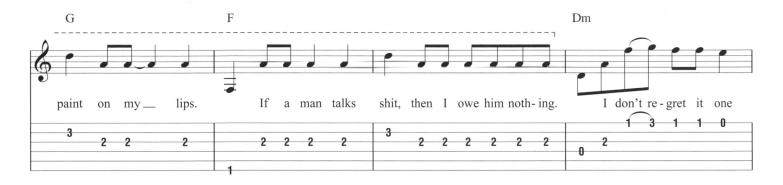

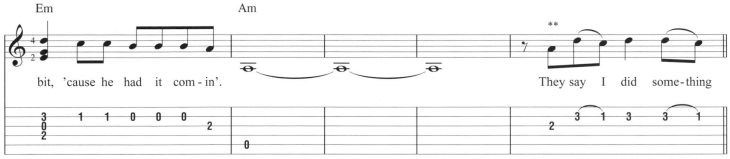

**Sung one octave higher thoughout Chorus.

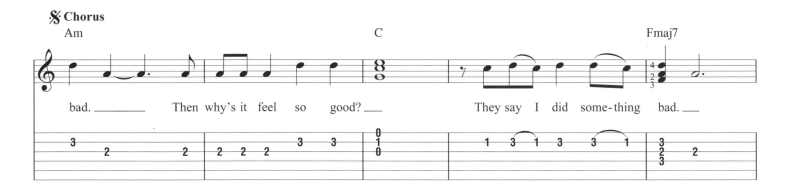

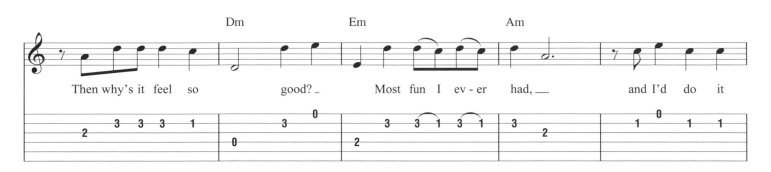

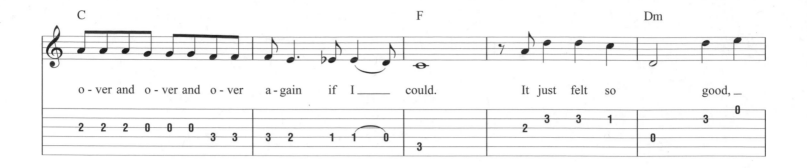

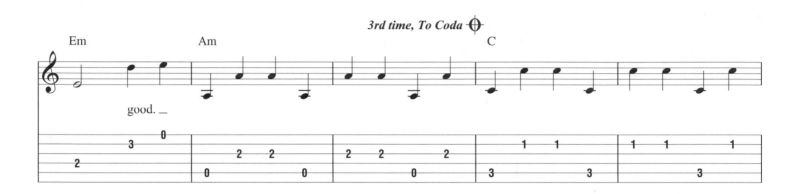

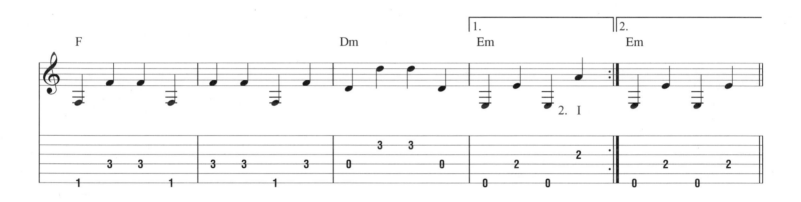

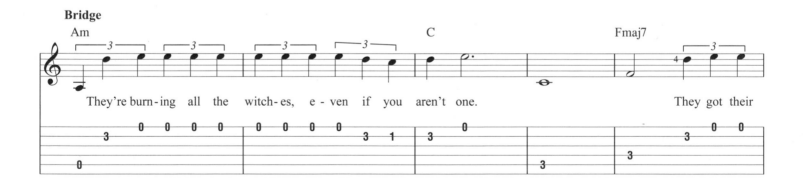

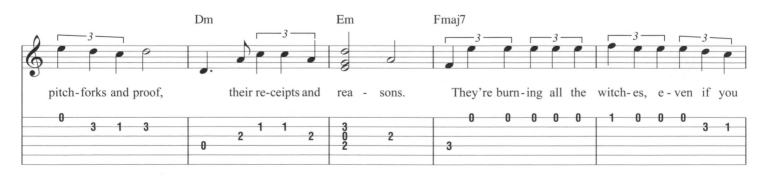

*Sung one octave higher.

Additional Lyrics

2. I never trust a playboy, but they love me.
So, I fly 'em all around the world and I let them think they saved me.
They never see it coming, what I do next.
This is how the world works. You gotta leave before you get left.
I can feel the flames on my skin.
He says, "Don't throw away a good thing."
But if he drops my name, then I owe him nothing.
And if he spends my change, then he had it comin'.

Don't Blame Me

Words and Music by Taylor Swift, Max Martin and Shellback

Strum Pattern: 5
Pick Pattern: 1

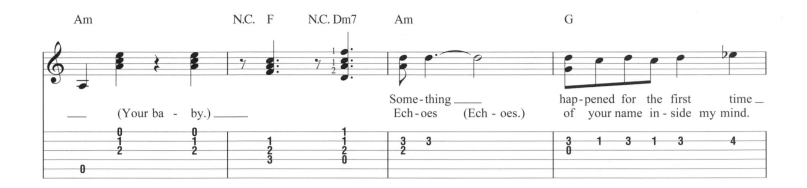

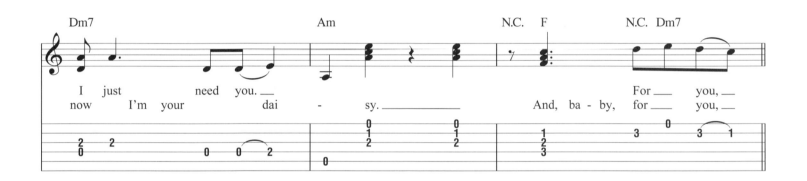

Pre-Chorus

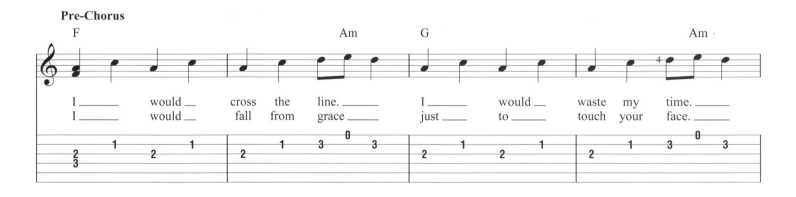

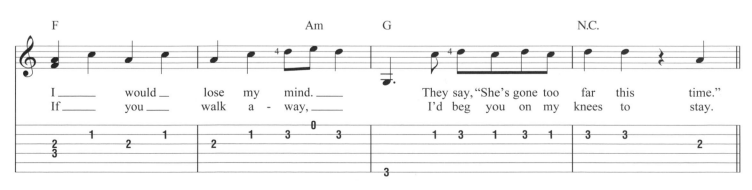

Don't blame me, love ____ made me cra-zy. If it does-n't, you ain't do-ing it ____ right. ____

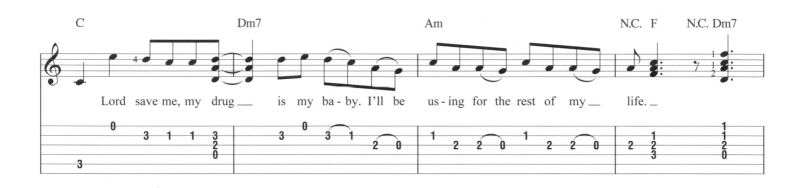

Lord save me, my drug ____ is my ba-by. I'll be us-ing for the rest of my ____ life. ____

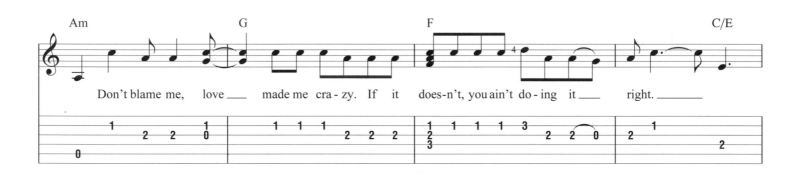

Don't blame me, love ____ made me cra-zy. If it does-n't, you ain't do-ing it ____ right. ____

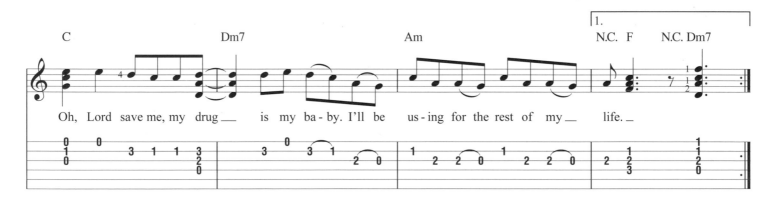

Oh, Lord save me, my drug ____ is my ba-by. I'll be us-ing for the rest of my ____ life. ____

Bridge — *To Coda* ⊕

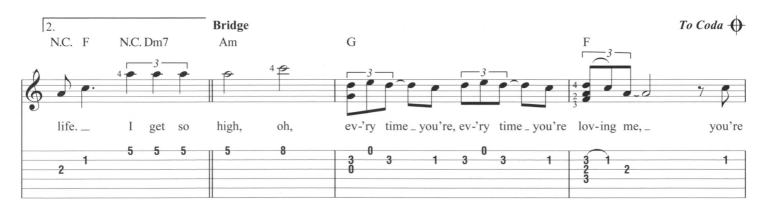

life. ____ I get so high, oh, ev-'ry time ____ you're, ev-'ry time ____ you're lov-ing me, ____ you're

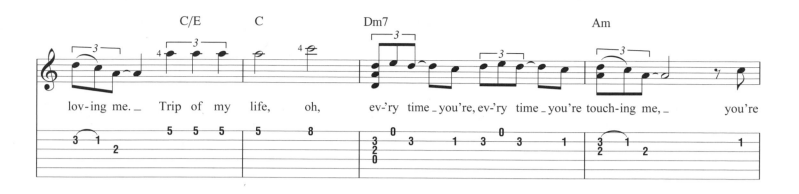

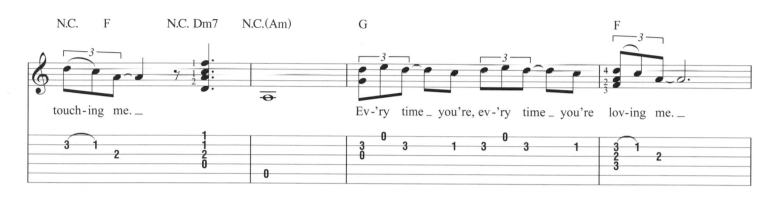

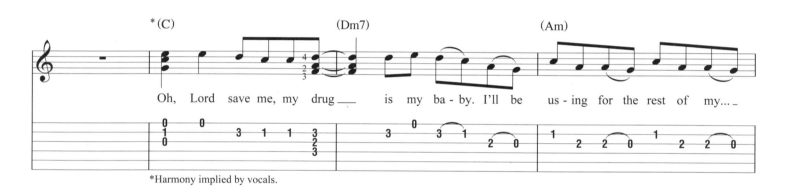

*Harmony implied by vocals.

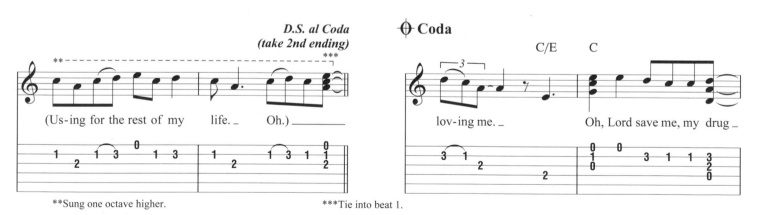

**Sung one octave higher.   ***Tie into beat 1.

Delicate

Words and Music by Taylor Swift, Max Martin and Shellback

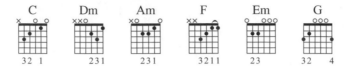

Strum Pattern: 3
Pick Pattern: 3

Intro
Moderately slow

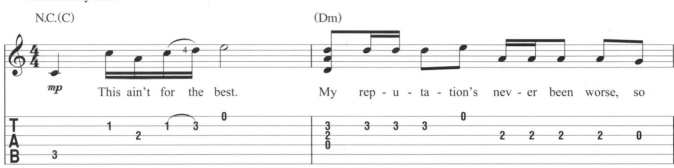

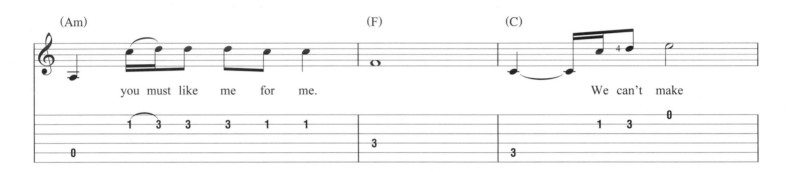

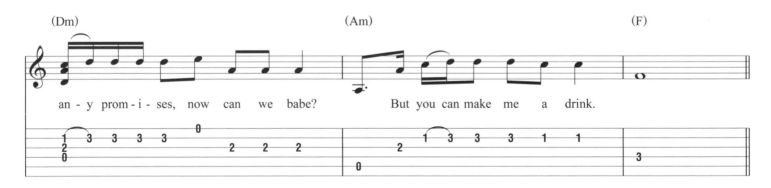

Verse

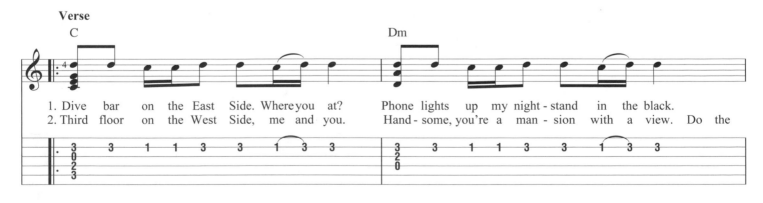

1. Dive bar on the East Side. Where you at? Phone lights up my night-stand in the black.
2. Third floor on the West Side, me and you. Hand-some, you're a man-sion with a view. Do the

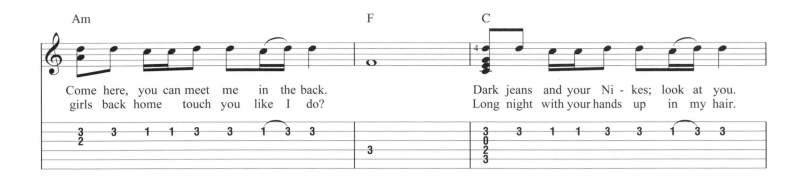

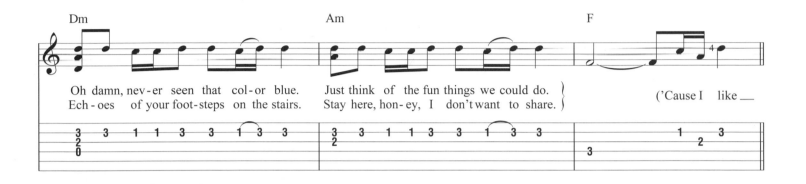

Pre-Chorus

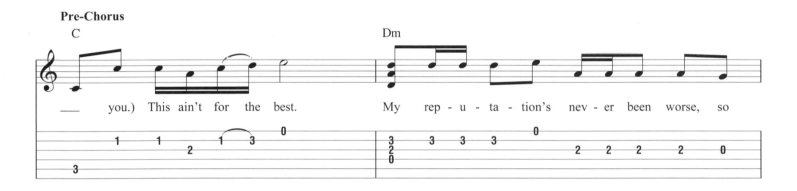

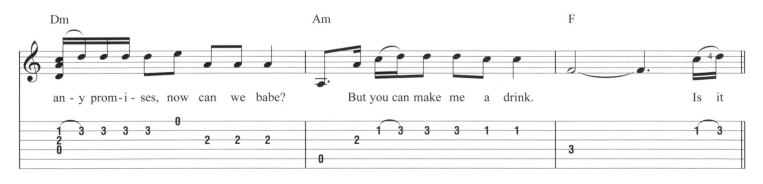

cool that I said all that? Is it chill that you're in my head? 'Cause I know that it's del - i - cate.

(Del - i - cate.) Is it cool that I said all that? Is it too soon to do this yet? 'Cause I

know that it's del - i - cate. Is - n't it, is - n't it, is - n't it, _____ is - n't it,

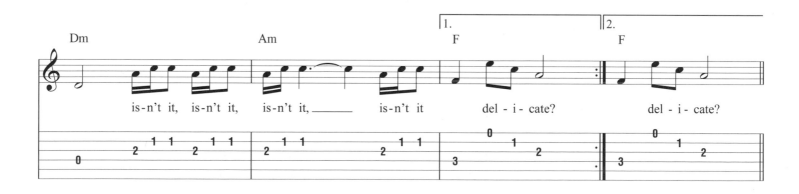

is - n't it, is - n't it, is - n't it, _____ is - n't it del - i - cate? del - i - cate?

Bridge

Some - times, I won - der _____ when you sleep, _____ are you ev - er dream -

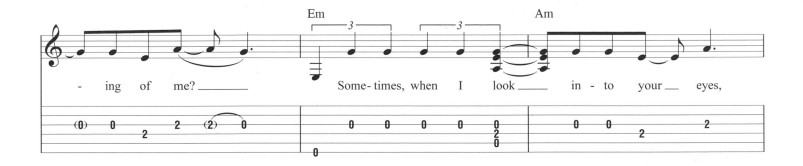

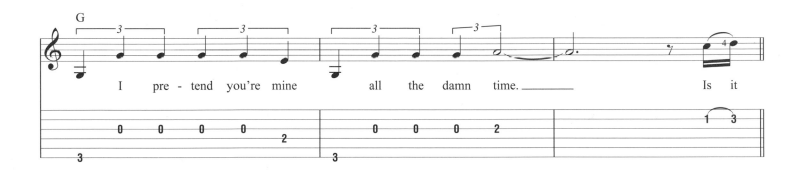

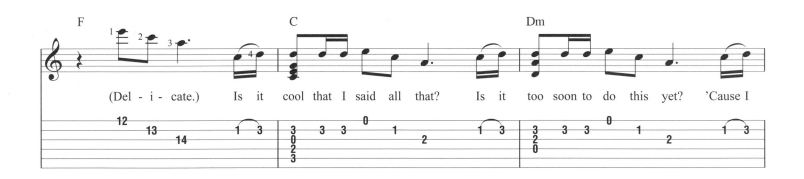

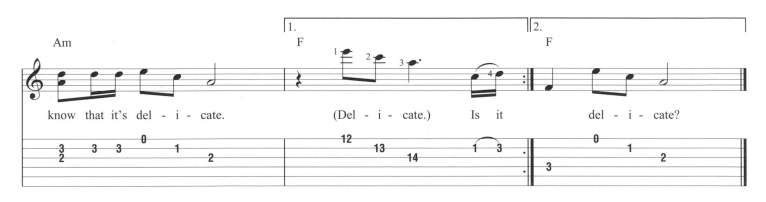

Look What You Made Me Do

Words and Music by Taylor Swift, Jack Antonoff, Richard Fairbrass, Fred Fairbrass and Rob Manzoli

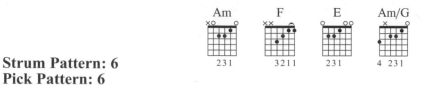

Strum Pattern: 6
Pick Pattern: 6

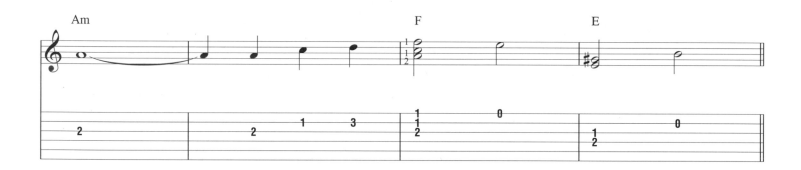

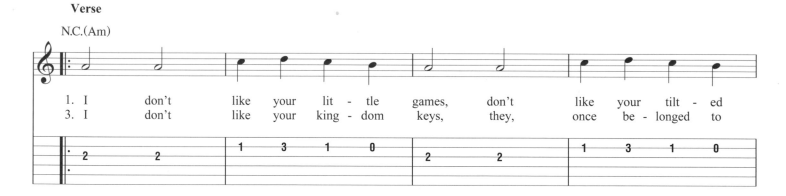

Verse

N.C.(Am)

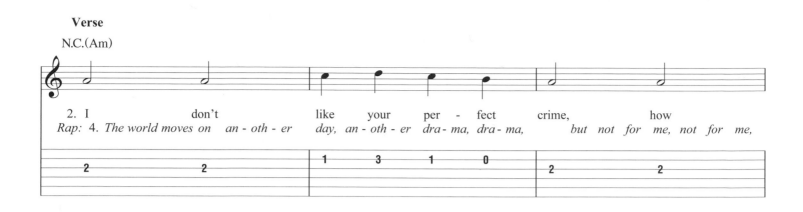

2. I don't like your per - fect crime, how
Rap: 4. The world moves on an - oth - er day, an - oth - er dra - ma, dra - ma, but not for me, not for me,

you laugh when you lie. You said the gun was
all I think a - bout is kar - ma. And then the world moves on, but one thing's for sure:

Pre-Chorus

Am

mine. Is - n't cool. No, I don't like you. But I got smart - er, I got
may - be I got mine but you'll all get yours.

Am/G

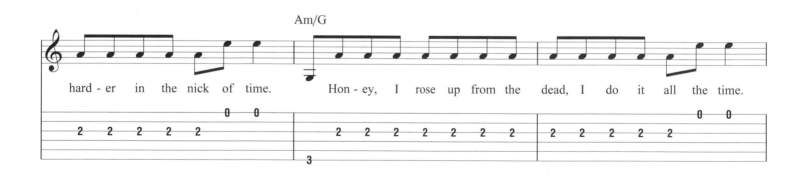

hard - er in the nick of time. Hon - ey, I rose up from the dead, I do it all the time.

F   E

I've got a list of names and yours is in red, un - der - lined. I check it once, then I

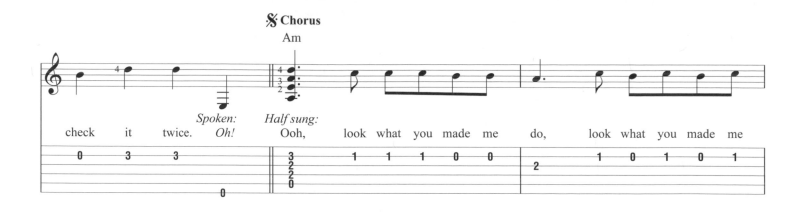

% **Chorus**

Am

Spoken: *Half sung:*

check it twice. *Oh!* Ooh, look what you made me do, look what you made me

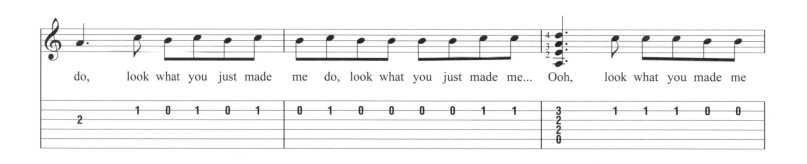

do, look what you just made me do, look what you just made me... Ooh, look what you made me

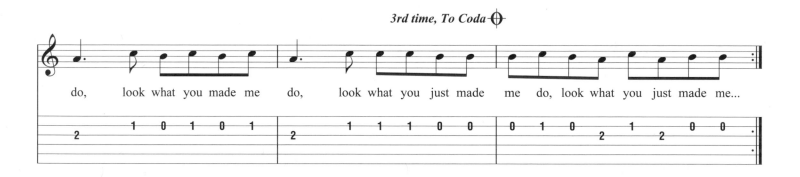

3rd time, To Coda ⊕

do, look what you made me do, look what you just made me do, look what you just made me...

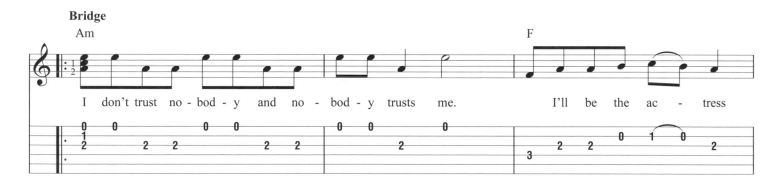

Bridge

Am   F

I don't trust no - bod - y and no - bod - y trusts me.   I'll be the ac - tress

‖1., 2., 3.   ‖4.   **Interlude**

E   E   Am

star - ring in your bad dreams.   star - ring in your bad dreams.

26

D.S. al Coda

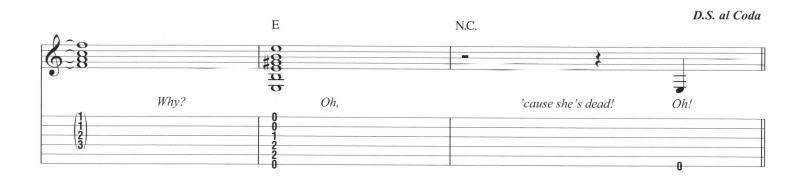

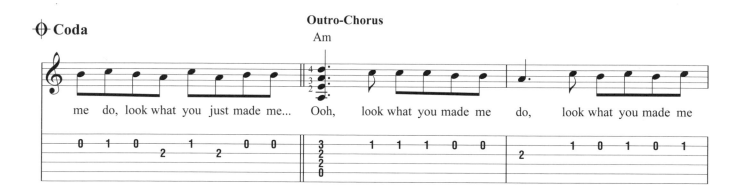

So It Goes...

Words and Music by Taylor Swift, Max Martin, Shellback and Oscar Gorres

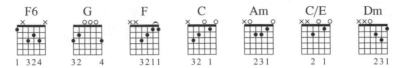

*Capo II

Strum Pattern: 1
Pick Pattern: 1

Verse
Moderately slow

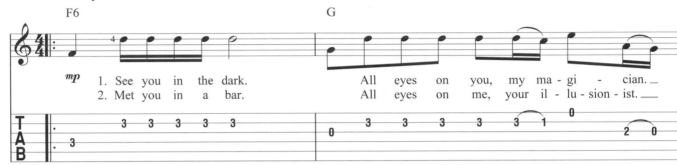

1. See you in the dark. All eyes on you, my ma-gi-cian. _
2. Met you in a bar. All eyes on me, your il-lu-sion-ist. __

*Optional: To match recording, place capo at 2nd fret.

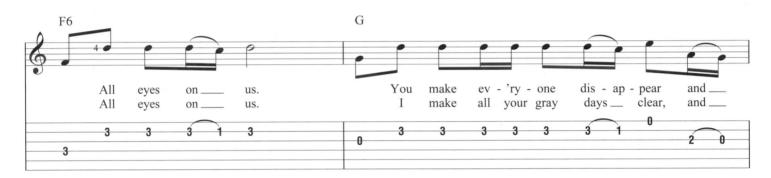

All eyes on __ us. You make ev-'ry-one dis-ap-pear and __
All eyes on __ us. I make all your gray days __ clear, and __

cut me in-to piec-es. __ Gold cage, hos-tage to my feel-ings. __
wear you like a neck-lace. __ I'm so chill, but you make me __ jeal-ous. __

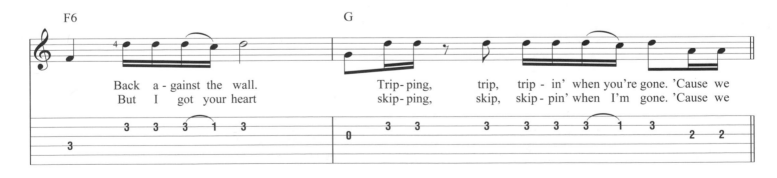

Back a-gainst the wall. Trip-ping, trip, trip-in' when you're gone. 'Cause we
But I got your heart skip-ping, skip, skip-pin' when I'm gone. 'Cause we

Pre-Chorus

break down a lit-tle, but when you get me a-lone, it's so sim-ple, 'cause ba-by,
break down a lit-tle, but when I get you a-lone, it's so sim-ple, 'cause ba-by,

I know what you know. We can feel it. _____ And all the
I know what you know. We can feel it. _____

𝄋 Chorus

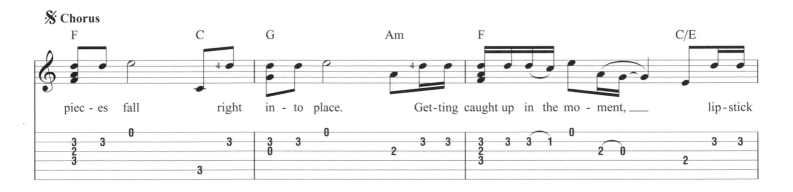

piec-es fall right in-to place. Get-ting caught up in the mo-ment, ___ lip-stick

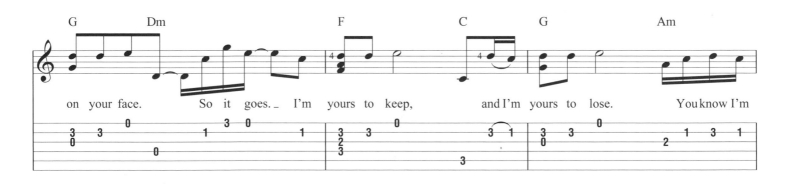

on your face. So it goes. _ I'm yours to keep, and I'm yours to lose. You know I'm

not a bad girl, but I ___ do bad things with you. So it goes. ___ Come here, _ dressed in black now.

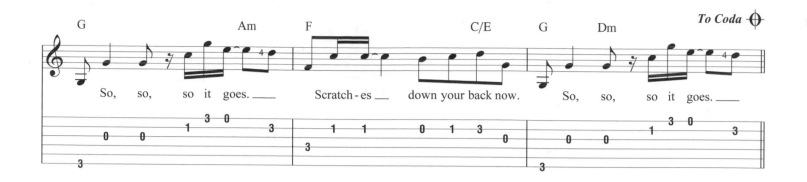

G   Am   F   C/E   G   Dm

So, so, so it goes. ___ Scratch-es ___ down your back now. So, so, so it goes. ___

Bridge

F6   G   F6

You did a ___ num-ber on me, but hon-est-ly, ba-by, who's count-ing? I did a ___ num-ber on

G   F6   G

you, but hon-est-ly, ba-by, who's count-ing? You did a ___ num-ber on me, but hon-est-ly, ba-by, who's count-ing?

D.S. al Coda (no repeat)   ⊕ **Coda**

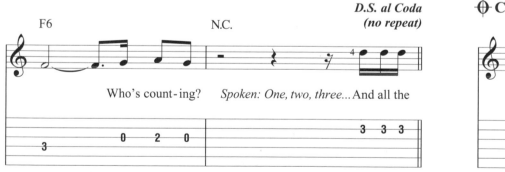 

F6   N.C.   F6

Who's count-ing? *Spoken: One, two, three...* And all the   Come here, _ dressed in black now.

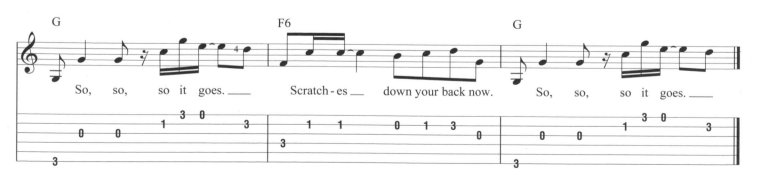

G   F6   G

So, so, so it goes. ___ Scratch-es ___ down your back now. So, so, so it goes. ___

Getaway Car

Words and Music by Taylor Swift and Jack Antonoff

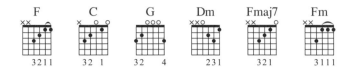

Strum Pattern: 3
Pick Pattern: 1

Intro
Fast
Half-time feel

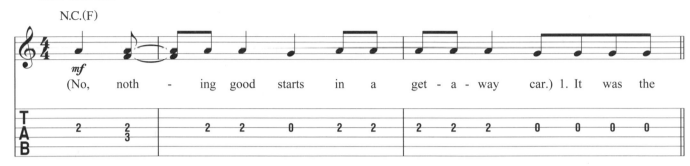

(No, noth - ing good starts in a get - a - way car.) 1. It was the

Verse

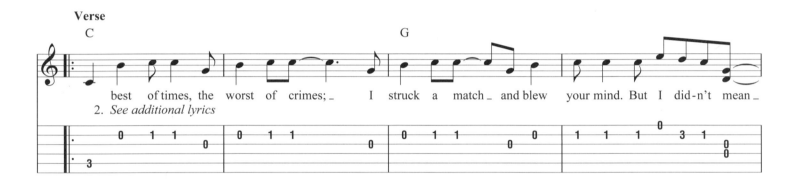

best of times, the worst of crimes; _ I struck a match _ and blew your mind. But I did-n't mean _
2. *See additional lyrics*

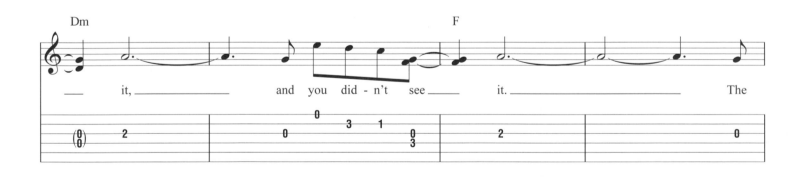

_ it, _____ and you did - n't see it. _____ The

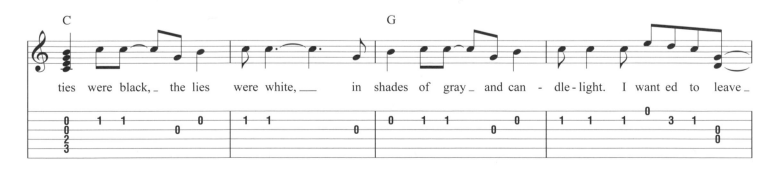

ties were black, _ the lies were white, ___ in shades of gray _ and can - dle-light. I want ed to leave _

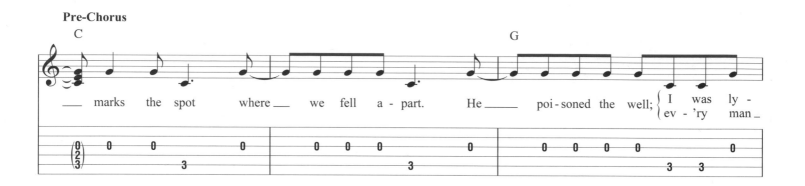

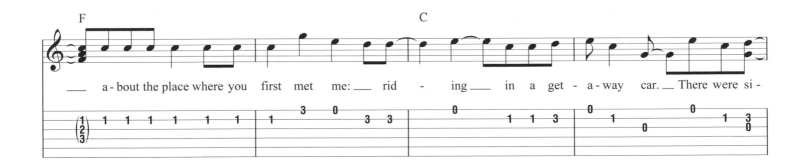

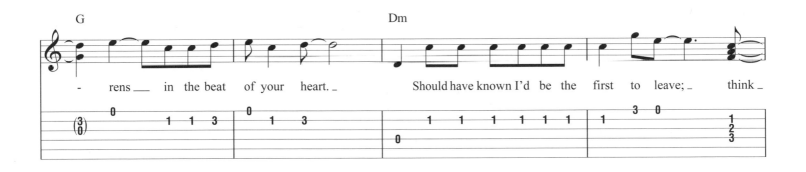

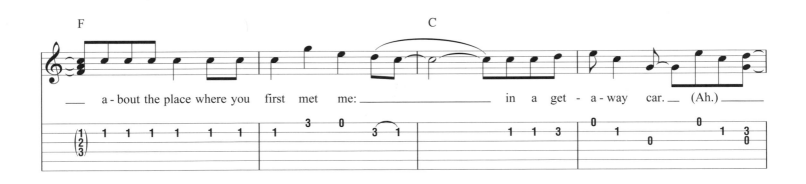

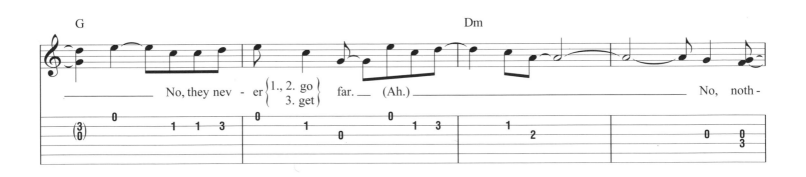

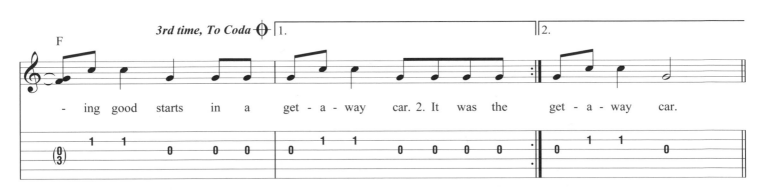

Bridge

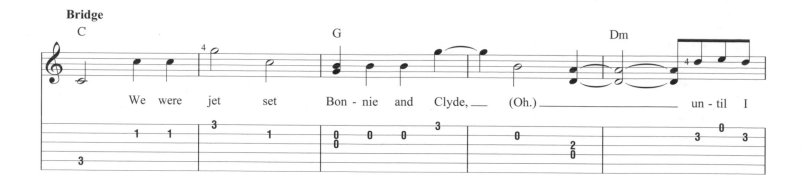

We were jet set Bon-nie and Clyde, ___ (Oh.) ___ un - til I

switched to the oth-er side, to the oth-er si - i - i - i - ide. It's no sur-prise I

turned you in, ___ (Oh.) ___ 'cause us trai - tors nev - er ___ win. ___

Chorus

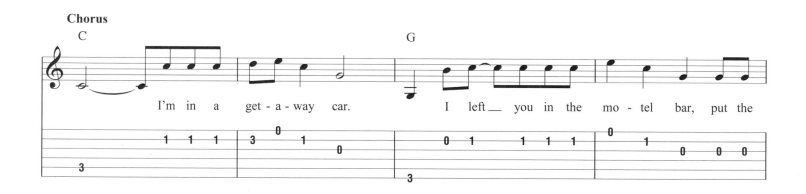

I'm in a get-a-way car. I left ___ you in the mo - tel bar, put the

D.S. al Coda

mon-ey in a bag and I stole the keys. ___ That ___ was the last time you ev - er saw me: driv-

⊕ Coda **Outro**

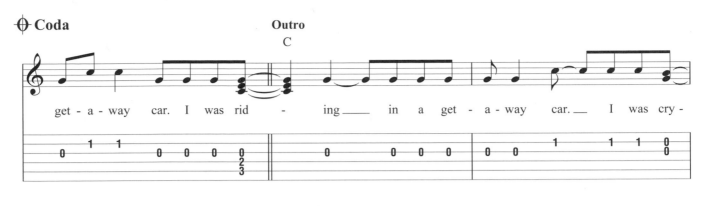

get - a - way   car. I was rid - ing ___ in a get - a - way   car. ___ I was cry -

- ing ___ in a get - a - way   car. ___ I was dy - ing ___ in a get -

a - way   car, ___ said, "Good - bye," ___ in ___ a   get - a - way   car. ___ Rid - ing ___ in a get -

a - way   car. ___ I was cry - ing ___ in a get - a - way   car. ___ I was dy - ing ___ in a get -

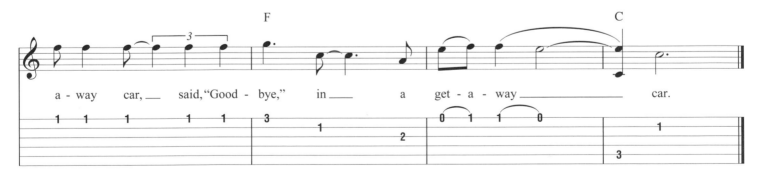

a - way   car, ___ said, "Good - bye," ___ in ___ a   get - a - way _____   car.

Additional Lyrics

2. It was the great escape, the prison break;
   The light of freedom on my face.
   But you weren't thinking, and I was just drinking.
   Well, he was running after us; I was screaming, "Go, go, go!"
   But with three of us, honey, it's a sideshow.
   And the circus ain't a love story; and now we're both sorry.
   (We're both sorry.)

Gorgeous

Words and Music by Taylor Swift, Max Martin and Shellback

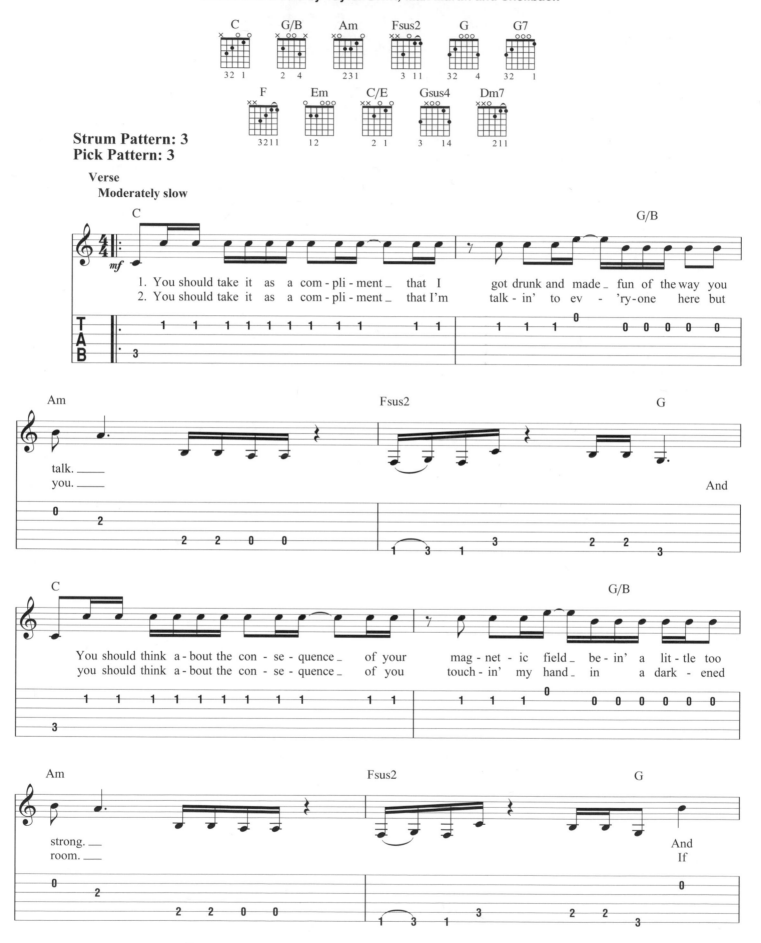

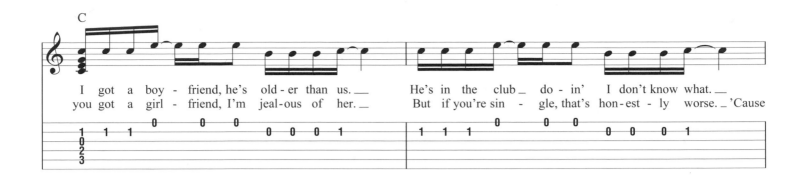

I got a boy - friend, he's old - er than us. ___ He's in the club ___ do - in' I don't know what. ___
you got a girl - friend, I'm jeal - ous of her. ___ But if you're sin - gle, that's hon - est - ly worse. ___ 'Cause

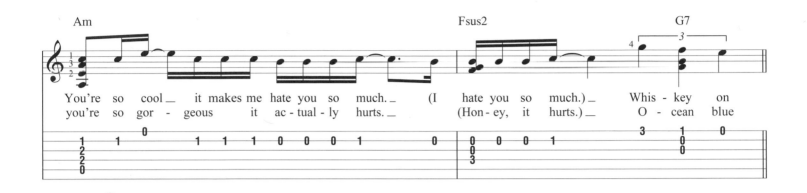

You're so cool ___ it makes me hate you so much. ___ (I hate you so much.) ___ Whis - key on
you're so gor - geous it ac - tual - ly hurts. ___ (Hon - ey, it hurts.) ___ O - cean blue

Pre-Chorus

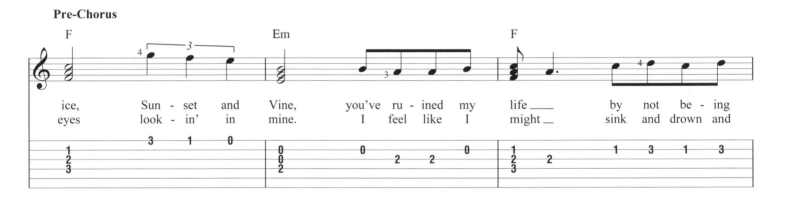

ice, Sun - set and Vine, you've ru - ined my life ___ by not be - ing
eyes look - in' in mine. I feel like I might ___ sink and drown and

𝄉 **Chorus**

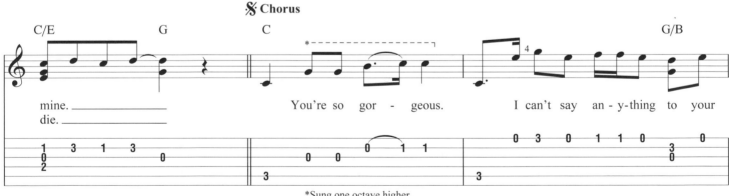

mine. ___ You're so gor - geous. I can't say an - y-thing to your
die. ___

*Sung one octave higher.

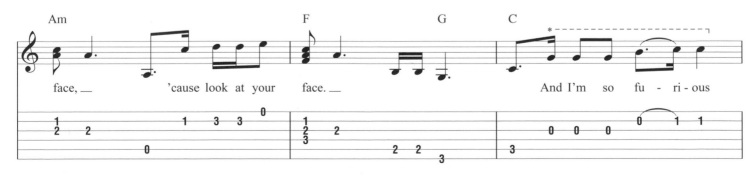

face, ___ 'cause look at your face. ___ And I'm so fu - ri - ous

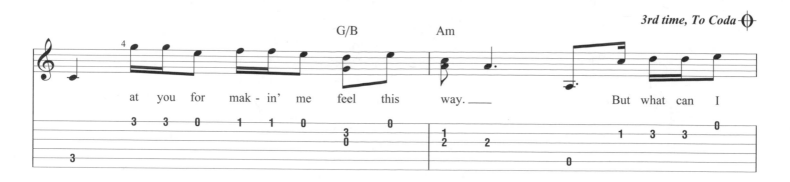

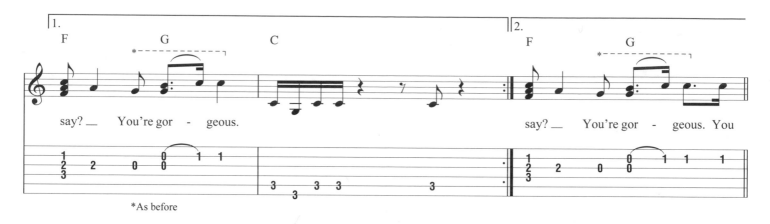

*As before

Bridge

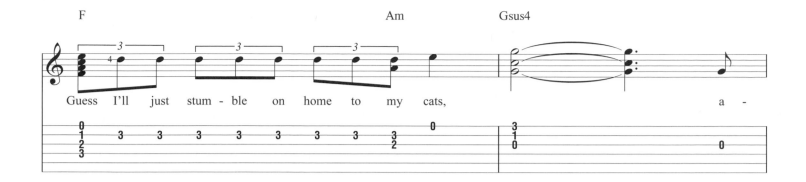

F   Am   Gsus4

Guess I'll just stum-ble on home to my cats,   a-

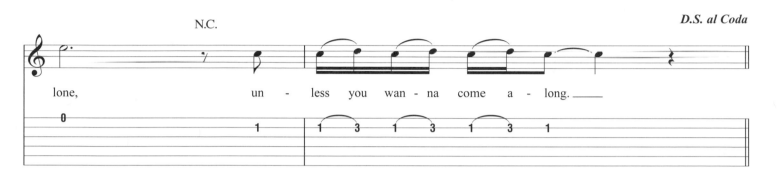

D.S. al Coda

N.C.

lone,   un - less you wan - na come a - long. _____

Coda   **Outro**

F   G   C

say? _____ You're gor - geous. You make me so hap - py it turns back to sad. There's

*As before

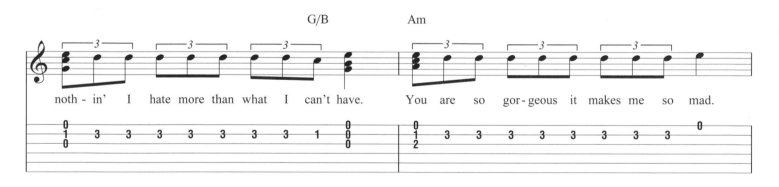

G/B   Am

noth - in' I hate more than what I can't have.   You are so gor - geous it makes me so mad.

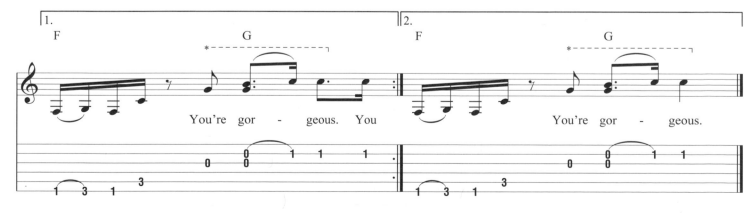

1.
F   G

You're gor - geous. You

2.
F   G

You're gor - geous.

King of My Heart

Words and Music by Taylor Swift, Max Martin and Shellback

Strum Pattern: 6
Pick Pattern: 6

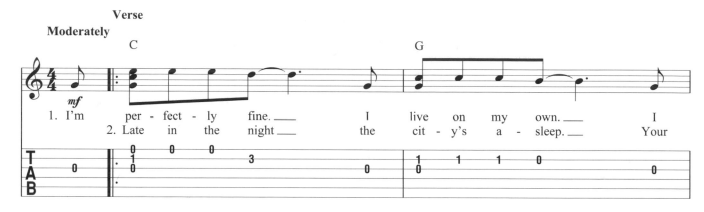

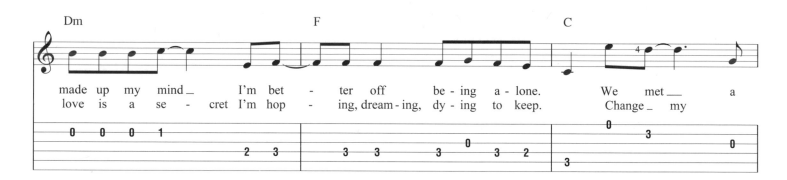

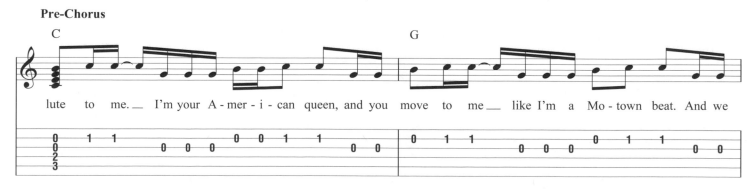

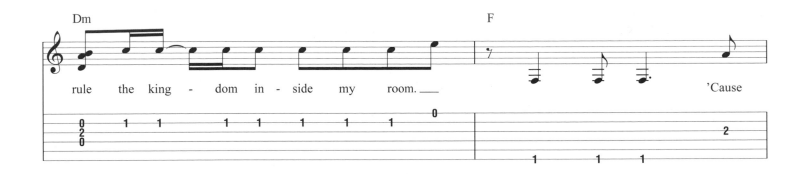

rule the king-dom in-side my room. ___ 'Cause

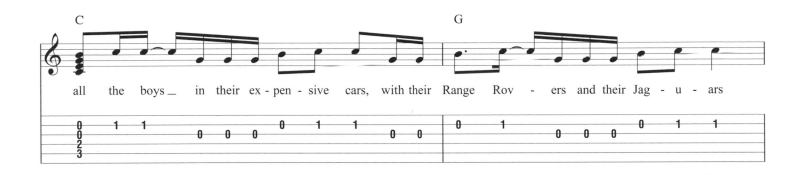

all the boys ___ in their ex-pen-sive cars, with their Range Rov-ers and their Jag-u-ars

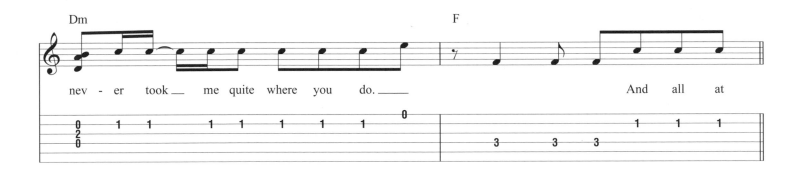

nev-er took ___ me quite where you do. ___ And all at

𝄋 Chorus

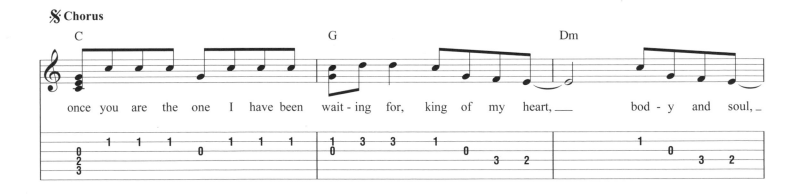

once you are the one I have been wait-ing for, king of my heart, ___ bod-y and soul, ___

___ ooh, oh. ___ And all at once you're all I want; I'll nev-er let you go, king of my heart, ___

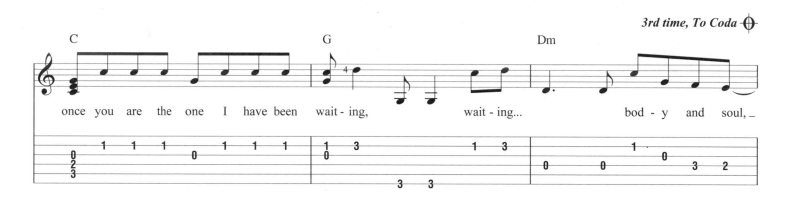

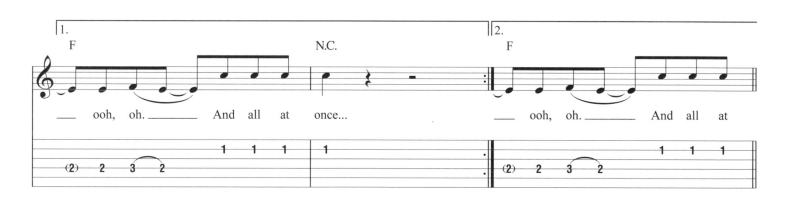

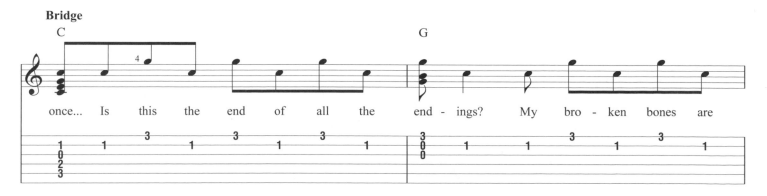

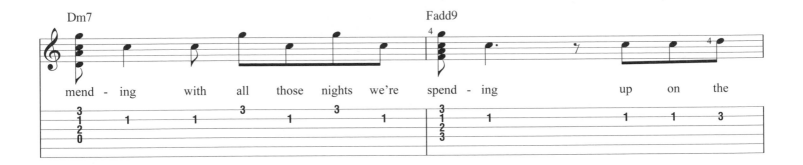

mend - ing   with   all   those   nights   we're   spend - ing   up   on   the

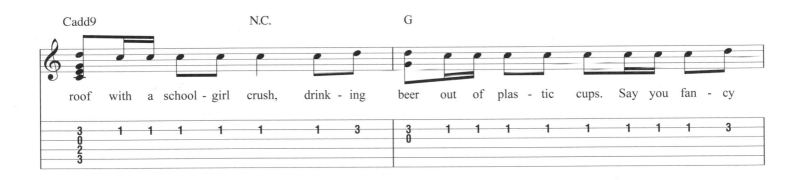

roof   with   a   school - girl   crush,   drink - ing   beer   out   of   plas - tic   cups.   Say   you   fan - cy

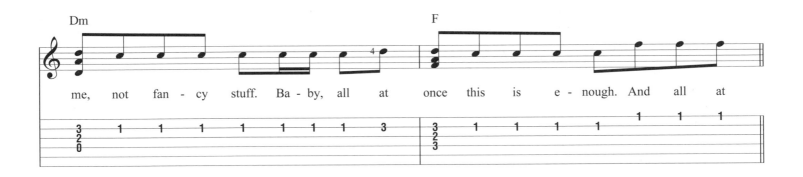

me,   not   fan - cy   stuff.   Ba - by,   all   at   once   this   is   e - nough.   And   all   at

Chorus

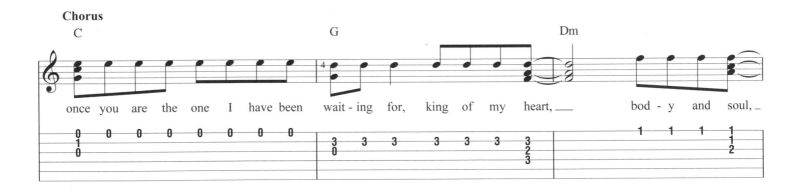

once   you   are   the   one   I   have   been   wait - ing   for,   king   of   my   heart, ___   bod - y   and   soul, ___

D.S. al Coda   ⊕ **Coda**

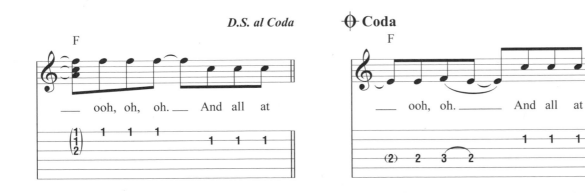

___   ooh,   oh,   oh. ___   And   all   at   ___   ooh,   oh. ___   And   all   at   once.

Dancing with Our Hands Tied

Words and Music by Taylor Swift, Max Martin, Shellback and Oscar Holter

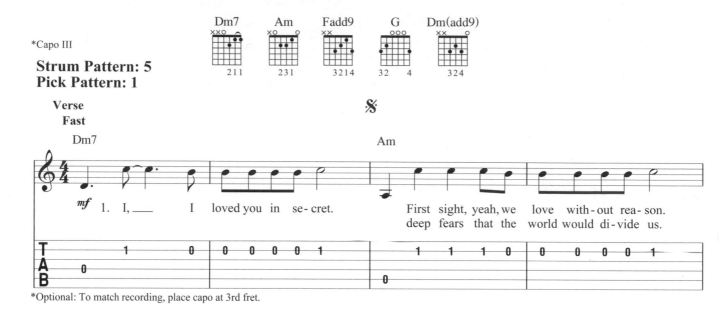

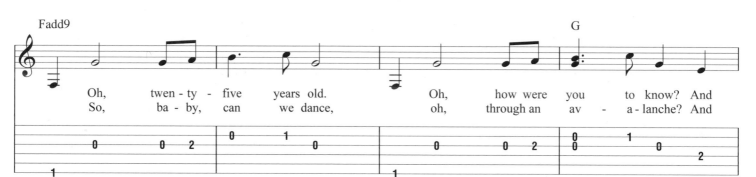

*Optional: To match recording, place capo at 3rd fret.

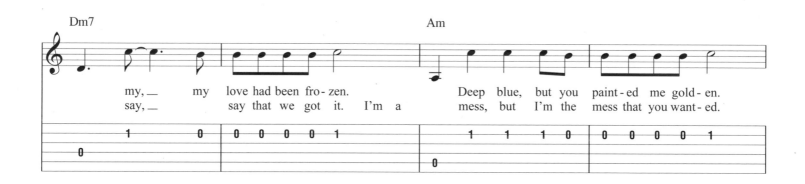

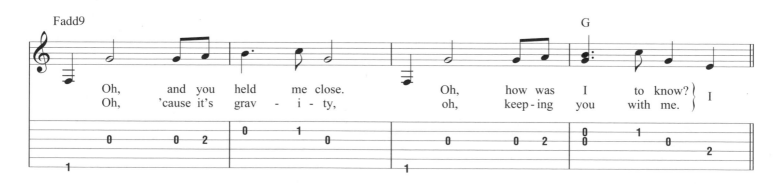

Pre-Chorus

Chorus
Half-time feel

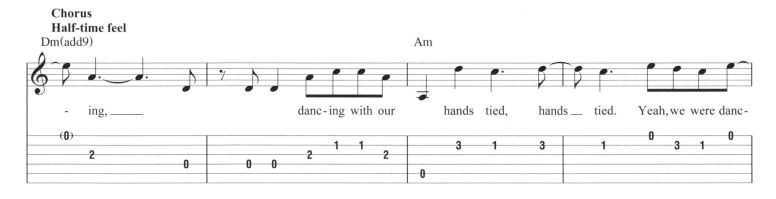

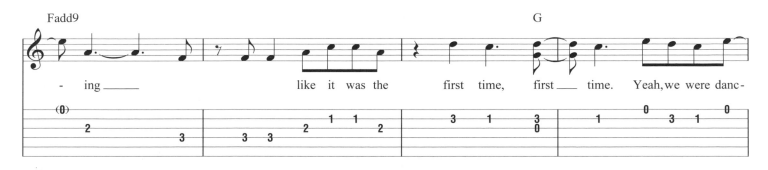

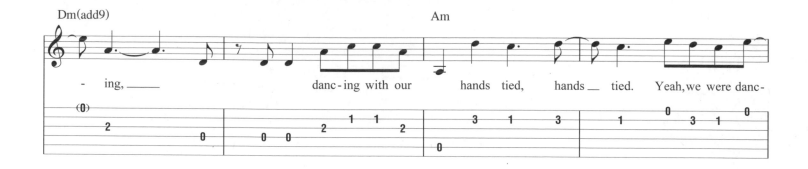

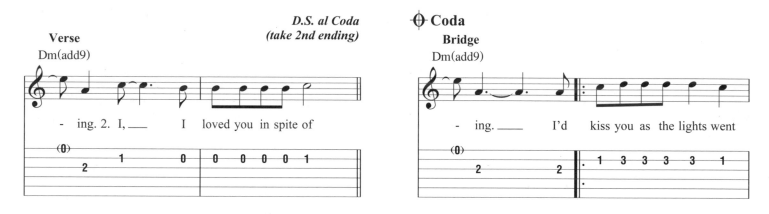

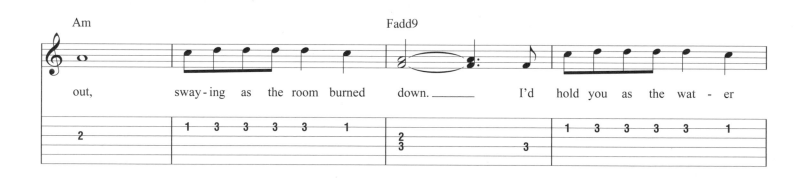

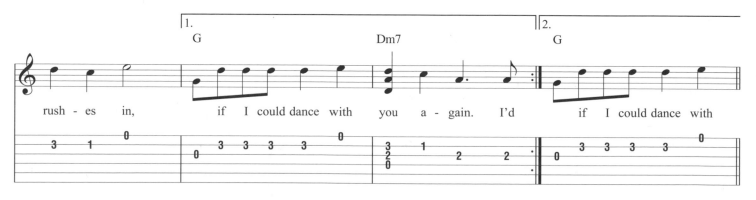

Chorus
Half-time feel

you a - gain.   Danc - ing with our   hands tied,   hands __ tied.   Yeah, we were danc-

1.

- ing _____   like it was the   first time,   first __ time.   Yeah, we were danc-

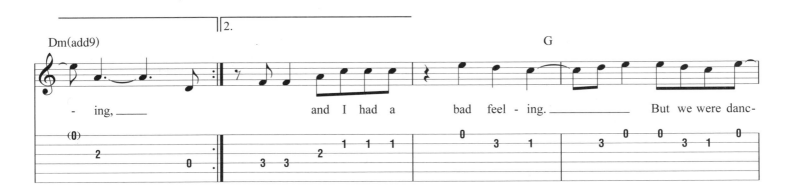

2.

- ing, _____   and I had a   bad feel - ing. _____   But we were danc-

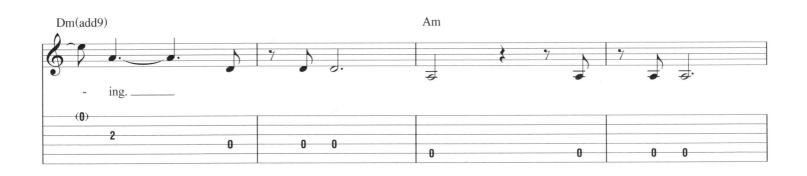

- ing. _____

Hands tied,   hands __ tied. _____

Dress

Words and Music by Taylor Swift and Jack Antonoff

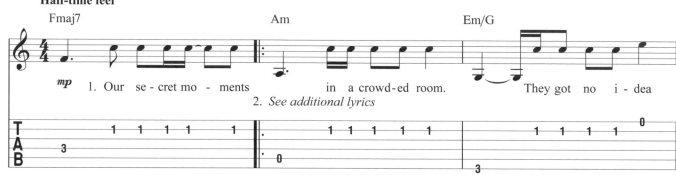

Strum Pattern: 3
Pick Pattern: 3

Verse
Moderately
Half-time feel

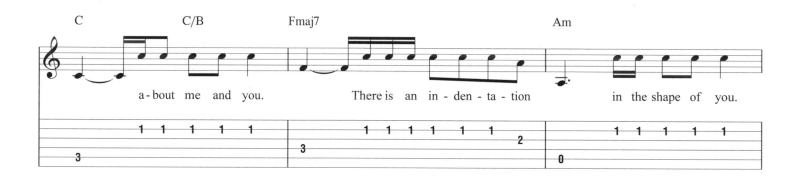

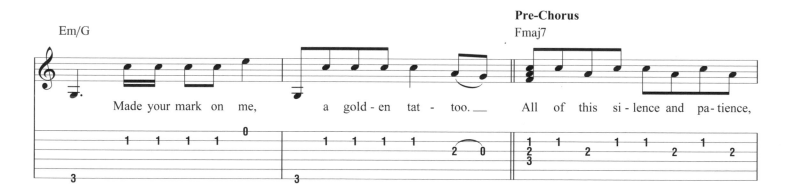

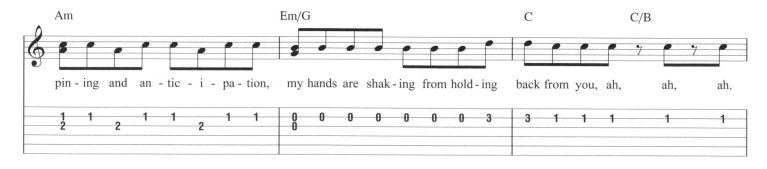

All of this si-lence and pa-tience, pin-ing and des-p'rate-ly wait-ing; my hands are shak-ing from all this

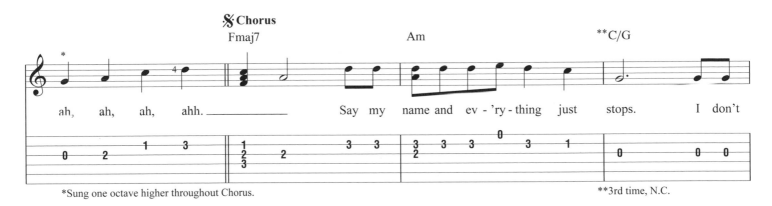

% Chorus

ah, ah, ah, ahh. _____ Say my name and ev-'ry-thing just stops. I don't

*Sung one octave higher throughout Chorus.

**3rd time, N.C.

want you like a best friend. On-ly bought this dress so you could take it off, take it

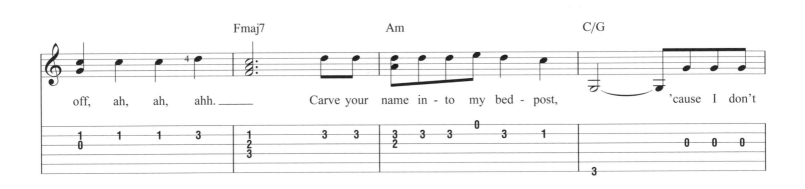

off, ah, ah, ahh. _____ Carve your name in-to my bed-post, 'cause I don't

3rd time, To Coda ⊕

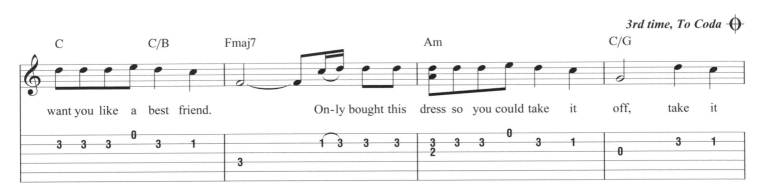

want you like a best friend. On-ly bought this dress so you could take it off, take it

49

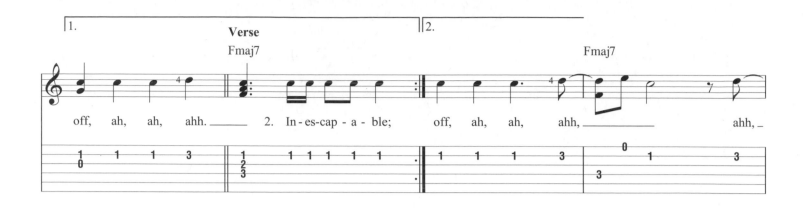

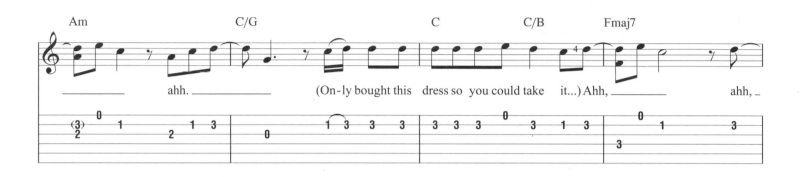

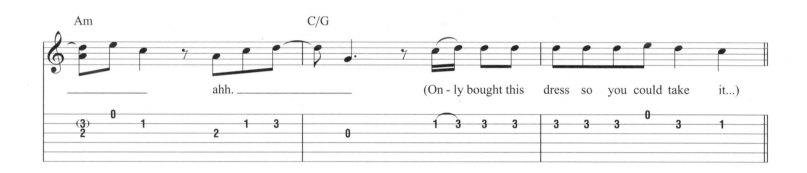

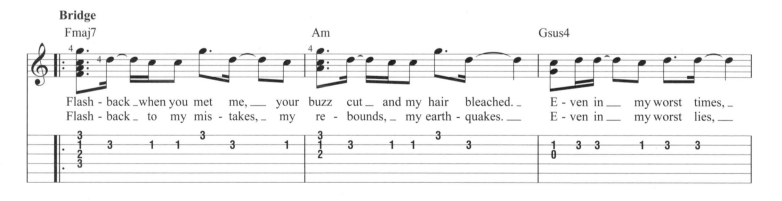

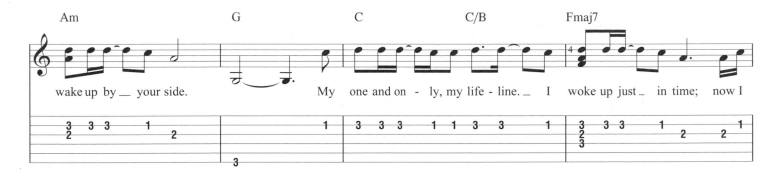

wake up by __ your side. My one and on - ly, my life - line. __ I woke up just __ in time; now I

D.S. al Coda

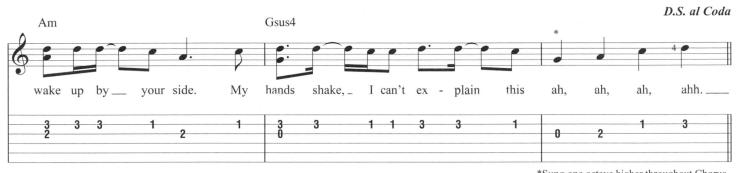

wake up by __ your side. My hands shake, __ I can't ex - plain this ah, ah, ah, ahh. __

*Sung one octave higher throughout Chorus.

Coda

Outro

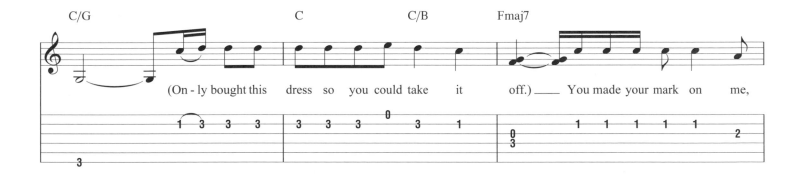

off, ah, ah, ahh. _____ There is an in - en - ta - tion in the shape of you.

(On - ly bought this dress so you could take it off.) __ You made your mark on me,

gold - en tat - too. (On - ly bought this dress so you could take it off.)

Additional Lyrics

2. Inescapable;
   I'm not even gonna try.
   And if I get burned, at least we were electrified.
   I'm spilling wine in the bathtub.
   You kiss my face, and we're both drunk.
   Ev'ryone thinks that they know us, but they know nothing about...

This Is Why We Can't Have Nice Things

Words and Music by Taylor Swift and Jack Antonoff

*Optional: To match recording, place capo at 3rd fret.

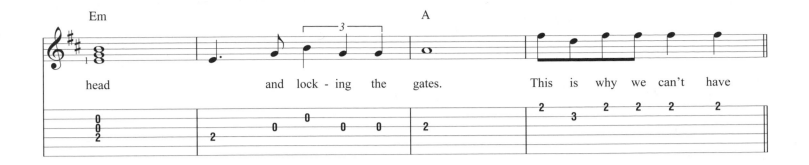

head and lock - ing the gates. This is why we can't have

%̤ Chorus

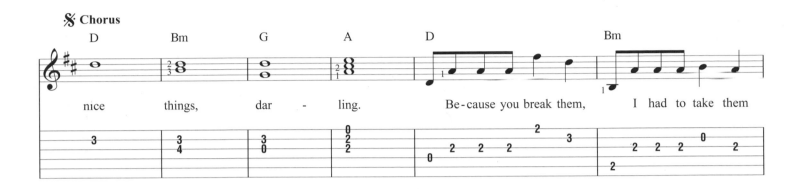

nice things, dar - ling. Be-cause you break them, I had to take them

a - way. ____ This is why we can't have nice things, hon - ey.

3rd time, To Coda ⊕

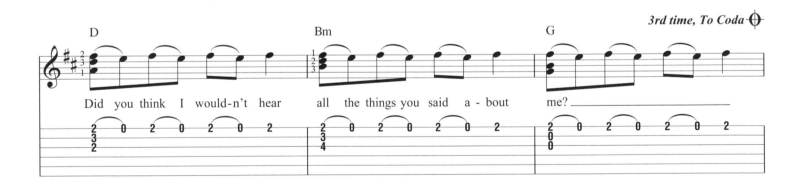

Did you think I would-n't hear all the things you said a - bout me? ____

This is why we can't have nice things. This is why we can't have...

Bridge

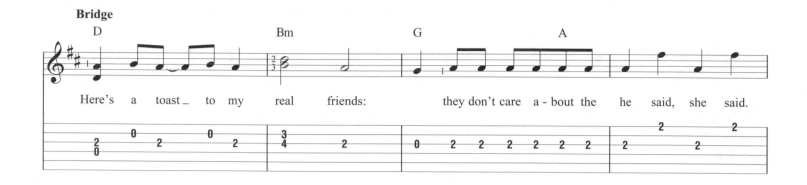

Here's a toast _ to my real friends: they don't care a-bout the he said, she said.

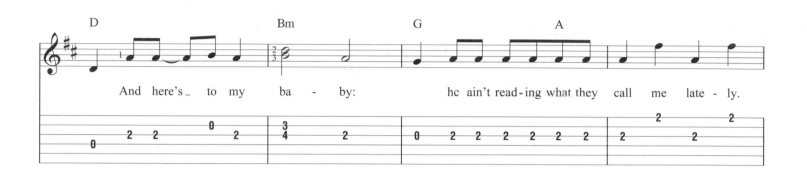

And here's _ to my ba — by: he ain't read-ing what they call me late-ly.

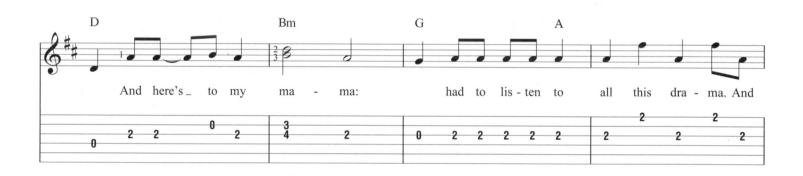

And here's _ to my ma — ma: had to lis-ten to all this dra-ma. And

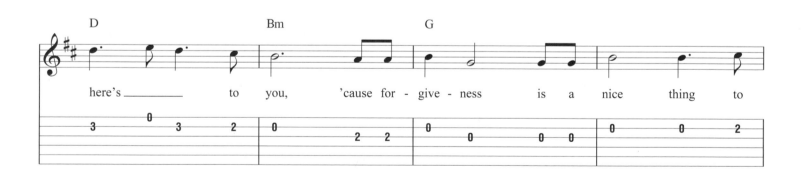

here's _____ to you, 'cause for-give-ness is a nice thing to

D.S. al Coda

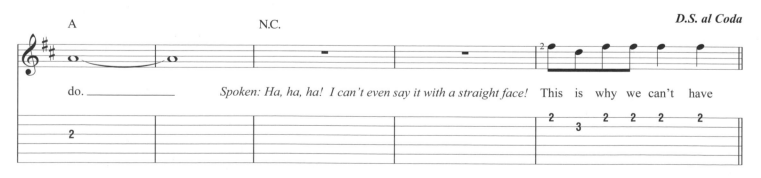

do. _____ *Spoken: Ha, ha, ha! I can't even say it with a straight face!* This is why we can't have

Additional Lyrics

2. It was so nice being friends again.
   There I was giving you a second chance,
   But you stabbed me in the back while shaking my hand.
   And therein lies the issue: friends don't try to trick you,
   Get you on the phone and mind-twist you.
   And so I took an axe to a mended fence.

Pre-Chorus But I'm not the only friend you've lost lately.
   If only you weren't so shady.

Call It What You Want

Words and Music by Taylor Swift and Jack Antonoff

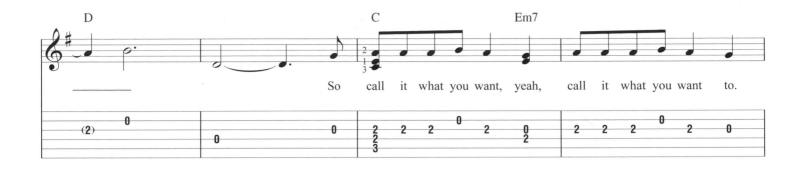

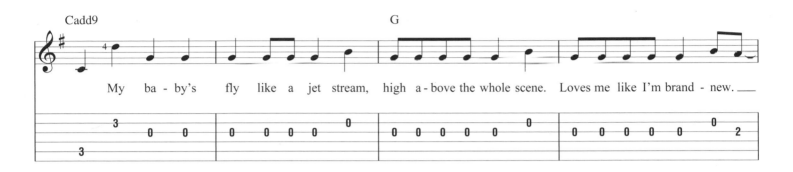

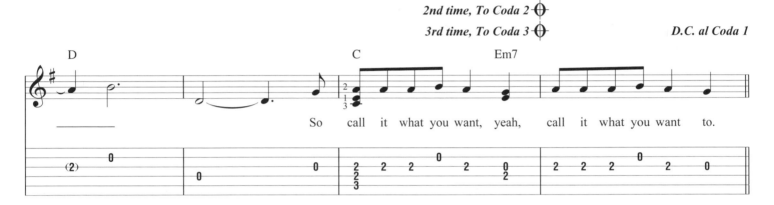

2nd time, To Coda 2 ⊕

3rd time, To Coda 3 ⊕

D.C. al Coda 1

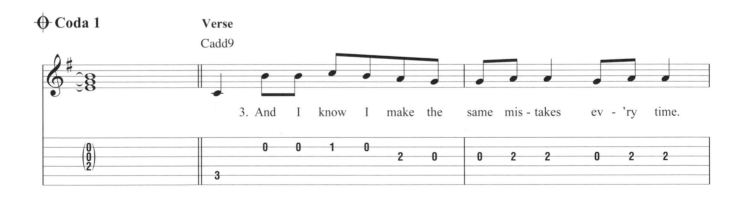

⊕ **Coda 1**   **Verse**

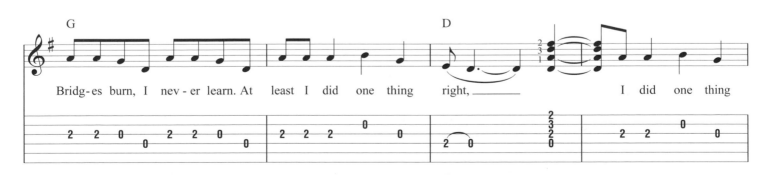

D.S. al Coda 2   ⊕ **Coda 2**

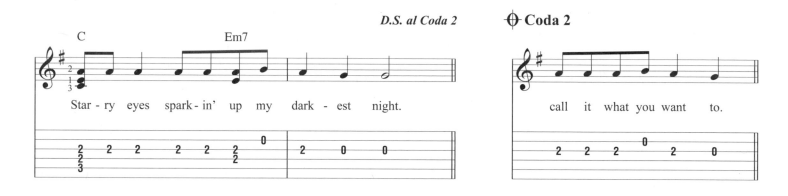

Bridge

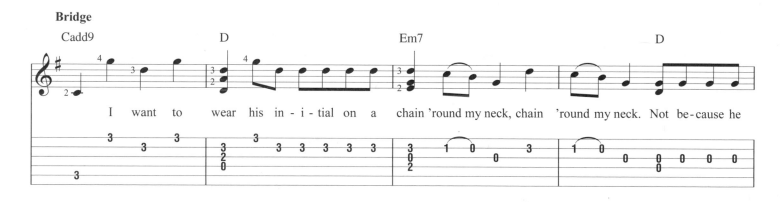

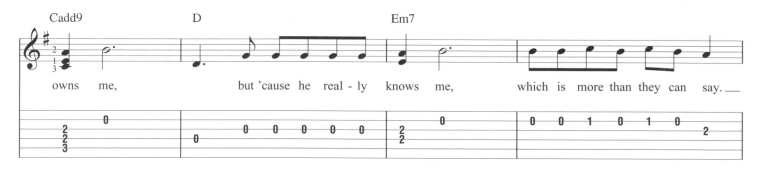

Additional Lyrics

2. All my flowers grew back as thorns.
   Windows boarded up after the storm.
   He built a fire just to keep me warm.
   All the drama queens takin' swings,
   All the jokers dressin' up as kings.
   They fade to nothin' when I look at him.

New Year's Day

Words and Music by Taylor Swift and Jack Antonoff

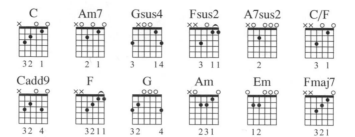

Strum Pattern: 3
Pick Pattern: 5

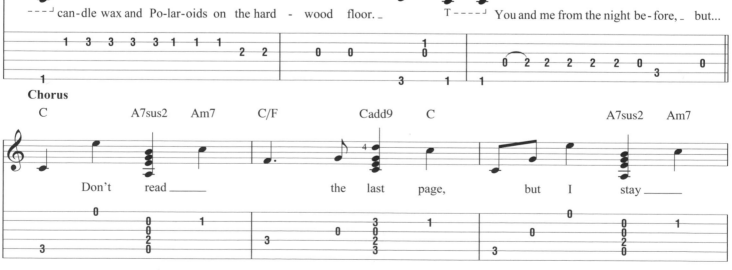

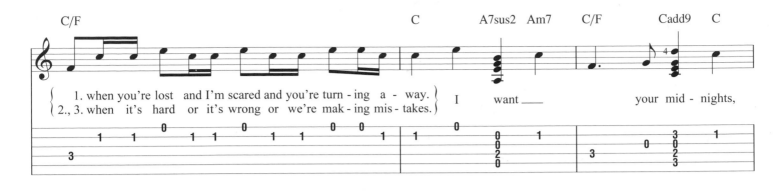

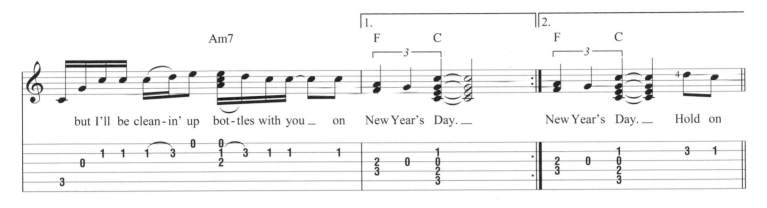

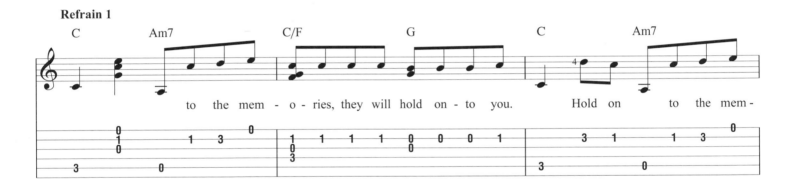

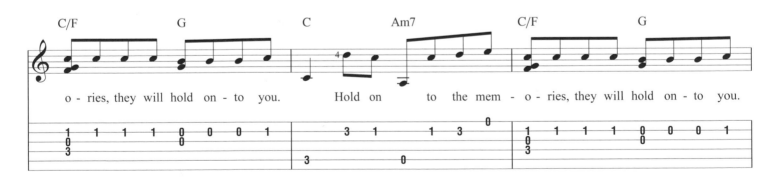

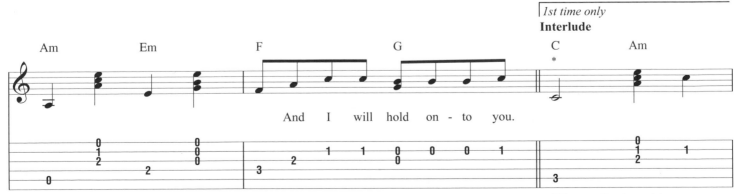

*Piano arr. for gtr., next 4 meas.

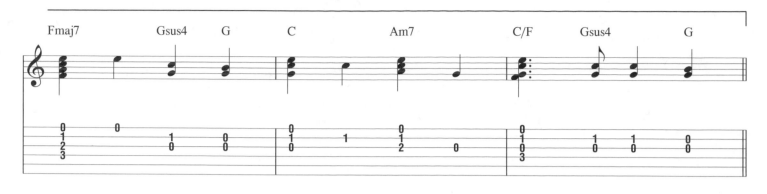

Refrain 2

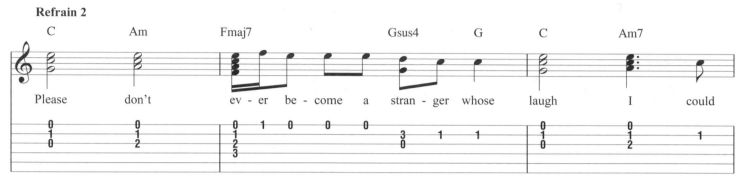

Please don't ev - er be - come a stran - ger whose laugh I could

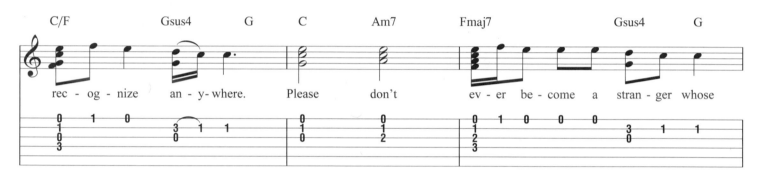

rec - og - nize an - y - where. Please don't ev - er be - come a stran - ger whose

To Coda ⊕

D.C. al Coda
(take 2nd ending)

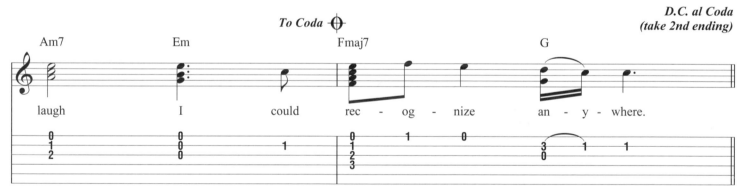

laugh I could rec - og - nize an - y - where.

⊕ **Coda**

Outro

Repeat and fade

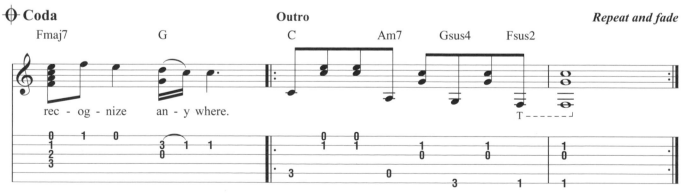

rec - og - nize an - y where.

Additional Lyrics

2. You squeeze my hand three times in the back of the taxi.
   I can tell that it's gonna be a long road.
   I'll be there if you're the toast of the town, babe,
   Or if you strike out and you're crawlin' home.

3. There's glitter on the floor after the party,
   Girls carrying their shoes down in the lobby,
   Candle wax and Polaroids on the hardwood floor.
   You and me forevermore.

EASY GUITAR
WITH NOTES & TAB

This series features simplified arrangements with notes, tab, chord charts, and strum and pick patterns.

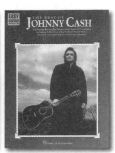

MIXED FOLIOS

00702287	Acoustic	$14.99
00702002	Acoustic Rock Hits for Easy Guitar	$14.99
00702166	All-Time Best Guitar Collection	$19.99
00699665	Beatles Best	$14.99
00702232	Best Acoustic Songs for Easy Guitar	$14.99
00119835	Best Children's Songs	$16.99
00702233	Best Hard Rock Songs	$14.99
00703055	The Big Book of Nursery Rhymes & Children's Songs	$14.99
00322179	The Big Easy Book of Classic Rock Guitar	$24.95
00698978	Big Christmas Collection	$16.95
00702394	Bluegrass Songs for Easy Guitar	$12.99
00703387	Celtic Classics	$14.99
00224808	Chart Hits of 2016-2017	$14.99
00702149	Children's Christian Songbook	$9.99
00702237	Christian Acoustic Favorites	$12.95
00702028	Christmas Classics	$8.99
00101779	Christmas Guitar	$14.99
00702185	Christmas Hits	$9.95
00702141	Classic Rock	$8.95
00702203	CMT's 100 Greatest Country Songs	$27.95
00702283	The Contemporary Christian Collection	$16.99

00702239	Country Classics for Easy Guitar	$19.99
00702282	Country Hits of 2009–2010	$14.99
00702257	Easy Acoustic Guitar Songs	$14.99
00702280	Easy Guitar Tab White Pages	$29.99
00702041	Favorite Hymns for Easy Guitar	$10.99
00140841	4-Chord Hymns for Guitar	$7.99
00702281	4 Chord Rock	$10.99
00126894	Frozen	$14.99
00702286	Glee	$16.99
00699374	Gospel Favorites	$14.95
00122138	The Grammy Awards® Record of the Year 1958-2011	$19.99
00702160	The Great American Country Songbook	$16.99
00702050	Great Classical Themes for Easy Guitar	$8.99
00702116	Greatest Hymns for Guitar	$10.99
00702130	The Groovy Years	$9.95
00702184	Guitar Instrumentals	$9.95
00148030	Halloween Guitar Songs	$14.99
00702273	Irish Songs	$12.99
00702275	Jazz Favorites for Easy Guitar	$15.99
00702274	Jazz Standards for Easy Guitar	$15.99
00702162	Jumbo Easy Guitar Songbook	$19.99
00702258	Legends of Rock	$14.99
00702261	Modern Worship Hits	$14.99

00702189	MTV's 100 Greatest Pop Songs	$24.95
00702272	1950s Rock	$15.99
00702271	1960s Rock	$15.99
00702270	1970s Rock	$15.99
00702269	1980s Rock	$14.99
00702268	1990s Rock	$14.99
00109725	Once	$14.99
00702187	Selections from O Brother Where Art Thou?	$14.99
00702178	100 Songs for Kids	$14.99
00702515	Pirates of the Caribbean	$12.99
00702125	Praise and Worship for Guitar	$10.99
00702285	Southern Rock Hits	$12.99
00121535	30 Easy Celtic Guitar Solos	$14.99
00702220	Today's Country Hits	$9.95
00121900	Today's Women of Pop & Rock	$14.99
00702294	Top Worship Hits	$15.99
00702255	VH1's 100 Greatest Hard Rock Songs	$27.99
00702175	VH1's 100 Greatest Songs of Rock and Roll	$24.95
00702253	Wicked	$12.99

ARTIST COLLECTIONS

00702267	AC/DC for Easy Guitar	$15.99
00702598	Adele for Easy Guitar	$15.99
00702040	Best of the Allman Brothers	$14.99
00702865	J.S. Bach for Easy Guitar	$14.99
00702169	Best of The Beach Boys	$12.99
00702292	The Beatles — 1	$19.99
00125796	Best of Chuck Berry	$14.99
00702201	The Essential Black Sabbath	$12.95
02501615	Zac Brown Band — The Foundation	$16.99
02501621	Zac Brown Band — You Get What You Give	$16.99
00702043	Best of Johnny Cash	$16.99
00702263	Best of Casting Crowns	$14.99
00702090	Eric Clapton's Best	$10.95
00702086	Eric Clapton — from the Album Unplugged	$10.95
00702202	The Essential Eric Clapton	$14.99
00702250	blink-182 — Greatest Hits	$15.99
00702053	Best of Patsy Cline	$12.99
00702229	The Very Best of Creedence Clearwater Revival	$15.99
00702145	Best of Jim Croce	$15.99
00702278	Crosby, Stills & Nash	$12.99
00702219	David Crowder*Band Collection	$12.95
14042809	Bob Dylan	$14.99
00702276	Fleetwood Mac — Easy Guitar Collection	$14.99
00130952	Foo Fighters	$14.99
00139462	The Very Best of Grateful Dead	$14.99
00702136	Best of Merle Haggard	$12.99
00702227	Jimi Hendrix — Smash Hits	$14.99
00702288	Best of Hillsong United	$12.99
00702236	Best of Antonio Carlos Jobim	$14.99

00702245	Elton John — Greatest Hits 1970–2002	$14.99
00129855	Jack Johnson	$14.99
00702204	Robert Johnson	$10.99
00702234	Selections from Toby Keith — 35 Biggest Hits	$12.95
00702003	Kiss	$10.99
00110578	Best of Kutless	$12.99
00702216	Lynyrd Skynyrd	$15.99
00702182	The Essential Bob Marley	$12.95
00146081	Maroon 5	$14.99
00121925	Bruno Mars – Unorthodox Jukebox	$12.99
00702248	Paul McCartney — All the Best	$14.99
00702129	Songs of Sarah McLachlan	$12.95
00125484	The Best of MercyMe	$12.99
02501316	Metallica — Death Magnetic	$17.99
00702209	Steve Miller Band — Young Hearts (Greatest Hits)	$12.95
00124167	Jason Mraz	$15.99
00702096	Best of Nirvana	$15.99
00702211	The Offspring — Greatest Hits	$12.95
00138026	One Direction	$14.99
00702030	Best of Roy Orbison	$14.99
00702144	Best of Ozzy Osbourne	$14.99
00702279	Tom Petty	$12.99
00102911	Pink Floyd	$16.99
00702139	Elvis Country Favorites	$12.99
00702293	The Very Best of Prince	$14.99
00699415	Best of Queen for Guitar	$14.99
00109279	Best of R.E.M.	$14.99
00702208	Red Hot Chili Peppers — Greatest Hits	$12.95

00174793	The Very Best of Santana	$14.99
00702196	Best of Bob Seger	$12.95
00146046	Ed Sheeran	$14.99
00702252	Frank Sinatra — Nothing But the Best	$12.99
00702010	Best of Rod Stewart	$16.99
00702049	Best of George Strait	$14.99
00702259	Taylor Swift for Easy Guitar	$15.99
00702260	Taylor Swift — Fearless	$14.99
00139727	Taylor Swift — 1989	$17.99
00115960	Taylor Swift — Red	$16.99
00253667	Taylor Swift — Reputation	$17.99
00702290	Taylor Swift — Speak Now	$15.99
00702226	Chris Tomlin — See the Morning	$12.95
00148643	Train	$14.99
00702427	U2 — 18 Singles	$14.99
00102711	Van Halen	$16.99
00702108	Best of Stevie Ray Vaughan	$14.99
00702123	Best of Hank Williams	$14.99
00702111	Stevie Wonder — Guitar Collection	$9.95
00702228	Neil Young — Greatest Hits	$15.99
00119133	Neil Young — Harvest	$14.99
00702188	Essential ZZ Top	$10.95

Prices, contents and availability subject to change without notice.

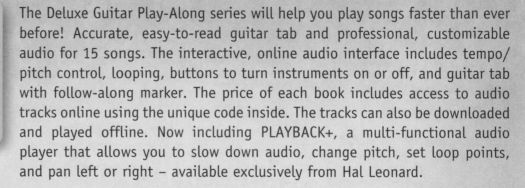

DELUXE GUITAR PLAY-ALONG

AUDIO ACCESS INCLUDED 🔊

The Deluxe Guitar Play-Along series will help you play songs faster than ever before! Accurate, easy-to-read guitar tab and professional, customizable audio for 15 songs. The interactive, online audio interface includes tempo/pitch control, looping, buttons to turn instruments on or off, and guitar tab with follow-along marker. The price of each book includes access to audio tracks online using the unique code inside. The tracks can also be downloaded and played offline. Now including PLAYBACK+, a multi-functional audio player that allows you to slow down audio, change pitch, set loop points, and pan left or right – available exclusively from Hal Leonard.

1. TOP ROCK HITS

Basket Case • Black Hole Sun • Come As You Are • Do I Wanna Know? • Gold on the Ceiling • Heaven • How You Remind Me • Kryptonite • No One Knows • Plush • The Pretender • Seven Nation Army • Smooth • Under the Bridge • Yellow Ledbetter.

00244758 Book/Online Audio $19.99

2. REALLY EASY SONGS

All the Small Things • Brain Stew • Californication • Free Fallin' • Helter Skelter • Hey Joe • Highway to Hell • Hurt (Quiet) • I Love Rock 'N Roll • Island in the Sun • Knockin' on Heaven's Door • La Bamba • Oh, Pretty Woman • Should I Stay or Should I Go • Smells Like Teen Spirit.

00244877 Book/Online Audio $19.99

3. ACOUSTIC SONGS

All Apologies • Banana Pancakes • Crash Into Me • Good Riddance (Time of Your Life) • Hallelujah • Hey There Delilah • Ho Hey • I Will Wait • I'm Yours • Iris • More Than Words • No Such Thing • Photograph • What I Got • Wonderwall.

00244709 Book/Online Audio $19.99

4. THE BEATLES

All My Loving • And I Love Her • Back in the U.S.S.R. • Don't Let Me Down • Get Back • A Hard Day's Night • Here Comes the Sun • I Will • In My Life • Let It Be • Michelle • Paperback Writer • Revolution • While My Guitar Gently Weeps • Yesterday.

00244968 Book/Online Audio $19.99

5. BLUES STANDARDS

Baby, What You Want Me to Do • Crosscut Saw • Double Trouble • Every Day I Have the Blues • Going Down • I'm Tore Down • I'm Your Hoochie Coochie Man • If You Love Me Like You Say • Just Your Fool • Killing Floor • Let Me Love You Baby • Messin' with the Kid • Pride and Joy • (They Call It) Stormy Monday (Stormy Monday Blues) • Sweet Home Chicago.

00245090 Book/Online Audio $19.99

6. RED HOT CHILI PEPPERS

The Adventures of Rain Dance Maggie • Breaking the Girl • Can't Stop • Dani California • Dark Necessities • Give It Away • My Friends • Otherside • Road Trippin' • Scar Tissue • Snow (Hey Oh) • Suck My Kiss • Tell Me Baby • Under the Bridge • The Zephyr Song.

00245089 Book/Online Audio $19.99

7. CLASSIC ROCK

Baba O'Riley • Born to Be Wild • Comfortably Numb • Dream On • Fortunate Son • Heartbreaker • Hotel California • Jet Airliner • More Than a Feeling • Old Time Rock & Roll • Rhiannon • Runnin' Down a Dream • Start Me Up • Sultans of Swing • Sweet Home Alabama.

00248381 Book/Online Audio $19.99

8. OZZY OSBOURNE

Bark at the Moon • Close My Eyes Forever • Crazy Train • Dreamer • Goodbye to Romance • I Don't Know • I Don't Wanna Stop • Mama, I'm Coming Home • Miracle Man • Mr. Crowley • No More Tears • Over the Mountain • Perry Mason • Rock 'N Roll Rebel • Shot in the Dark.

00248413 Book/Online Audio $19.99

9. ED SHEERAN

The A Team • All of the Stars • Castle on the Hill • Don't • Drunk • Galway Girl • Give Me Love • How Would You Feel (Paean) • I See Fire • Lego House • Make It Rain • Perfect • Photograph • Shape of You • Thinking Out Loud.

00248439 Book/Online Audio $19.99

www.halleonard.com